MW01442983

Mastering the Art of Success: Unleashing Leadership Competency, Retention, Enrollment to Completion

Author: Dr. Samuel E. Said
Reviewer: Dr. Abbas Imam

Contents

Forward 5
Introduction 8
Leadership Development 11
    Planning Professional Development for Faculty 12
    Characteristics of an educational leader 15
    Productivity 18
    Intentional Mindfulness 20
    Decluttering our mind 21
    Leadership Development Pressures 21
What is leadership competency? 24
    Develop Leadership Competencies? 26
    Criteria for Practical Competency Model? 28
    Leadership time implication 28
    Transformational Leadership 31
Leadership Competencies 34
    Competency 1 - Integrity 35
        Leading with integrity 36
    Competency 2 - Accountability 39
        Clear accountability language. 40
    Competency 3 - Authenticity 42
        How do you develop authenticity? 43
    Competency 4 – Compassion 44
    Competency 5 – Wisdom 46
    Competency 6 – Inspiration 48
    Competency 7 – Vision 49
    Competency 8 – Conflict management 49
        Problem-solving 52

- Competency 9 – Innovation 58
- Competency 10 – Organizational Awareness 59
- Competency 11 – Discipline 60
- Competency 12 – Adaptability 62

Student successful journey 64
- Successful Transition from High School to College/University 64
- Student's Mindset for Academic Success: Cultivating a Growth Mindset 67
- Student Success 69

Retention 73
- Internal Factors 74
  - Students' Inward Battles 75
  - Faculty and Institution Mindset 78
- Solutions and strategies 83
- Strategies 84
  - Promoting Student engagements 84
- Goals 86
- Action plans 87
- Success Experience Course 88
  - Course Goal 88
  - Course Overview 88
  - Student Learning Outcomes 89
  - Course Objectives 90
  - The student's statement of purpose 91
  - Scheduled academic adviser's meetings 91
  - Create Good Habits 91
  - Consideration 92

Strategies to increase the effectiveness in enrollment, retention, and completion of Information Technology academic programs 94

Deliver education, training, and certification credentials to develop the most competitive workforce. 94

Increase enrollment of students in career and technical courses and programs through customized corporate training 94

Ensure a high level of IT enrollment, retention, and completion....................95

Alignment of credit and noncredit courses as a stepping stone to additional education and training that leads to higher earnings and greater career sustainability 96

ENROLLMENT—Creating Opportunities 97

Early Recruitment Activities 98

Personalize student communications 98

Involve Parents and guardians in the college search. 99

Make the students, not our college, the focal point of our recruitment messaging 100

Integrating media strategy 100

Digital Advertising 101

Search Engine Optimization (SEO)...101

Measurement, Reporting, and Optimization 102

Dual enrollment..102

Increased competitions 102

Capitalizing on dual enrollment rebounds 103

Increased unmet basic needs & mental health concerns 103

Pell Grant availability for incarcerated adults 104

A shrinking talent market...104

Completion 104

Completion of Student progression. 106

Connection from Interest in Application Strategies 106

Entry from Enrollment to Completion of Success Courses..................107

4

Progress from entry into Course of Study to 75% of requirements completed 107
Completion of a program of study to credential with labor market value. ...108
Engagement 108
Student to Students Engagement 108
Student-Faculty Engagement 110
References 113

Forward

In the ever-evolving landscape of education, the challenges of retention and completion in our educational institutions have emerged as critical issues that demand thoughtful and strategic solutions. As we navigate these complexities, the role of practical leadership competencies has become increasingly apparent. This book comprehensively explores the vital relationship between leadership competencies and student retention and completion rates—a timely and essential contribution to education.

It draws from empirical research and real-world experiences. This book delves into the integral connection between leadership and student success. It illuminates the profound impact of skilled and empathetic leaders on fostering a supportive and inclusive learning environment. At its core, this book highlights a crucial truth: leadership competencies are not merely abstract concepts but powerful tools that can shape the destiny of educational institutions and the students they serve

Throughout these pages, readers will encounter an invaluable exploration of key leadership competencies that can significantly influence retention and completion rates. Solid communication skills, empathetic engagement, proactive problem-solving, and strategic decision-making are among them. The authors eloquently illustrate how these competencies can create a sense of belonging, promote student success initiatives, and provide essential support and resources to enhance student engagement and persistence.

An essential aspect of this book is its emphasis on collaborative efforts to address retention challenges. It advocates for leaders to work with faculty, staff, and other stakeholders to implement retention-focused strategies and initiatives. The significance of data-driven decision-making and continuous assessment is highlighted as instrumental in identifying areas for improvement and developing targeted interventions. They are acknowledging the multifaceted factors influencing student retention and completion. This book offers a comprehensive perspective. From financial constraints and academic challenges to personal circumstances, it underscores the need for leaders to cultivate a student-centered culture. By supporting academic advising and mentoring programs and embracing innovative approaches to enhance student learning and success, leaders can drive transformative change within their institution.

In conclusion, this book is an indispensable resource for educators, administrators, and anyone passionate about student success. It illuminates the critical role of leadership competencies in tackling the challenges of retention and completion head-on. By cultivating leaders with these competencies, educational institutions can pave the way for initiatives that foster a supportive environment, ensuring every student has the opportunity to thrive and complete their educational journey successfully.

As you embark on this insightful journey through the pages that follow, may this book inspire and equip you with the knowledge and tools to make a lasting impact on the lives of students and the educational community at large.

Dr. Samuel E. Said

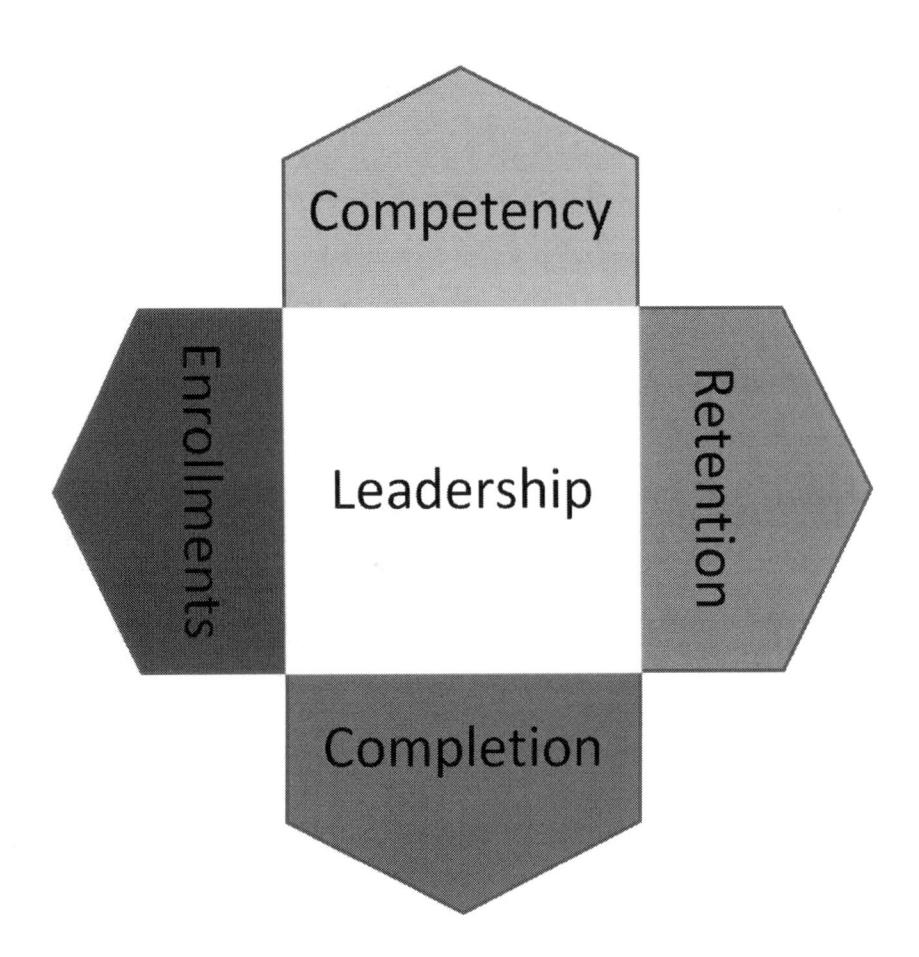

```
            Competency

Enrollments  Leadership  Retention

            Completion
```

Introduction

The success of any institution, educational or otherwise, depends on its leadership effectiveness and success. Leaders are learners; influential leaders have a toolbox full of skills, abilities, and competencies that make them a benchmark of success. Therefore, educational institutions must develop leadership programs to enhance their leaders' effectiveness.

According to DDIWoods Global Leadership Forecast 2021 (Development Dimensions International, Inc., 2020), 40% of leaders do not have a written or up-to-date development plan. Therefore leaders feel unprepared for the challenges of their roles and increasingly overwhelmed, confused, and stressed about their roles.

Nothing destroys morals more quickly and entirely than the feeling that those in authority do not know their mind. Incompetent leaders have countless opportunities to demonstrate their ineffectiveness by doing nothing wrong. Incompetence wears down credibility, which in turn erodes trust and loyalty. The result is most often ugly and disruptive.

Most leaders suffer from self-deception, and they are not aware of it. An infant is learning how to crawl. The infant begins by pushing himself back around the house. Backing their body around, he gets lodged beneath the furniture. The infant thrashes about, crying and banging their little head against the sides and footings of the pieces. The infant is stuck and hates it. So the only thing the infant can think of is how to get out— The infant pushes even harder, which worsens the problem. The infant is more stuck than ever (The Arbinger Institute, 2018).

If this infant could talk, he would blame the furniture for his troubles. After all, he is doing everything he can imagine. The problem could not be his. However, of course, the problem is his, even though he cannot see it. While it is true that he is doing everything he can think of, the problem is that he cannot see how he is the problem. Having the trouble he has, nothing he can think of will be a solution (The Arbinger Institute, 2018).

Self-deception is like a germ that kills leadership effectiveness and teamwork, a germ that causes many 'people problems,' an embryo that can be isolated and neutralized. This germ causes disease, and like child fever, self-deception has many different symptoms—from lack of motivation and commitment to stress and communication problems (The Arbinger Institute, 2018).

Leaders act from one of two positions: a peaceful heart or a heart at conflict and war with themselves and others. Operating on competencies from a spirit of peace produces a unifying fruit, fulfilling the institution's vision, goals, and values. Nevertheless, working on competencies from the heart of war creates conflicting outcomes that lead to division, dissatisfaction, and a destructive, stressful environment.

Self-awareness is the ability to understand and be aware of one's heart condition. It requires a high level of honesty in dealing with self-assessment. For this reason, many leaders are self-deceived because of the intuitive nature of this skill.

Self-deception in leadership is the cause of most problems in higher education; we teach and encourage leaders to concentrate on self-development, forgetting that they are a crucial part of a living organism. In a world of unprecedented business complexities, leaders, besides explicit knowledge, need an inner compass of self-awareness to walk the tightrope of leadership. Transformative leadership guided by the outward mindset impacts how we see the world as it is, not how we imagine it.

Overcoming the biggest impediment to mindset change:

1. Apply the outward-mindset pattern: See the needs, objectives, and challenges of others; Adjust efforts to be more helpful to others; Measure and hold yourself accountable for the impact of work on others

2. Do not wait for others to change. An essential move is to turn our mindset regardless of whether others change theirs.

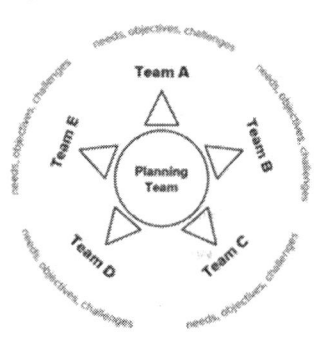

3. Mobilize the college to achieve a collective goal. Each person is part of a larger whole.

4. Allow people to be fully responsible. Own their work, plans, actions, and impact and position others to own theirs.

5. Eliminate the unnecessary differences that create distance between college leadership.

6. Rethink systems and processes to turn them outward; create an organizational ecosystem that energizes people rather than manages objects (The Arbinger Institute, 2018).

The outward -Mindset

Many leaders do not recognize what competencies they need, where to look for them, and how to develop and use them. Most of these situations arise because of their lack of knowledge and awareness of their job description, supervisors'

Leadership development *isn't* one-size-fits-all. Designing experiences that match the moment the leader is experiencing can create a **breakthrough** moment.

expectations, and the importance of fulfilling their institution's vision, values, Goals, and strategic plan. Most solutions to most of these problems are simple (training and development). Leadership development must be a career-long endeavor of constant improvement, not a one-time event. Planned development must be personalized to leaders' needs to maximize the effectiveness of the time invested in their development.

Leadership is not a position but a human venture inevitably filled with challenges, triumphs, and failures. Behind every leadership role is a person trying to do their best in an environment of changing expectations and uncertainty. Therefore, educational institutions must focus on supporting their leaders through critical leadership moments. These moments are crucial leadership transformative moments that transition from an employment's parturition to a new leadership level.

Leadership is about mobilizing others to want to struggle for shared aspirations and make great things happen. (Kouzes & Posner, 2019)" Leaders do not possess all the competencies needed to run a corporation. The effort of teamwork, competencies, and the ability to collaborate in the movement of living organisms toward accomplishing the desired outcome fulfills the vision of the collective. The writer lives by this rule of thumb and always hires people more competent than themselves; why? Because we all are smart together? The fundamental truth is that leaders never make extraordinary things happen alone."

Leadership Development

Leadership development has never been more essential to anticipating, navigating, and solving higher education's complex challenges. Young people struggle to find their place in life and face many challenges. Lack of proper guidance, leadership training, and mentoring causes them to fall into severe unexpected consequences given by adequate higher education leadership.

Leadership aims to help our faculty and students grow and develop. It is vital to the success of any educational department. There is a link between the leadership we provide and our teams' performance. We must understand that leadership is not a position but a place where skills and competencies thrive for productivity, effectiveness, and success.

There is power in our words. The words from the leader's mouth give the listeners life. Whether the created life is good or bad depends on the spoken words and the perceived understanding of such words. Leaders should not hasten to give answers to questions has not been thoroughly thought out.

Leaders must acknowledge that all leaders have a moment of weakness and are astray by their goals and values. Blaming others for failure rather than accepting responsibility is unhealthy for their team's livelihood and learning experiences.

Leadership development is a lifelong process; it has no end. Its excellence thrives through the continued development of competencies with specific skills and abilities; therefore, Leaders must embrace growth.

Planning Professional Development for Faculty.

Developing a professional development plan for faculty involves assessing their needs, setting goals, providing resources and support, and evaluating progress. Here's a step-by-step guide to creating an effective professional development plan:

- **Assess Needs**: Conduct a needs assessment to identify the areas where faculty members require professional development. This can be done through surveys, interviews, focus groups, or performance evaluations. Gather feedback on specific skills, knowledge gaps, teaching methodologies, technology integration, research, or other relevant areas.
- **Set Goals**: Based on the needs assessment, establish clear and specific goals for each faculty member. Goals should align with their roles, responsibilities, and career aspirations. Ensure that the goals are realistic, measurable, and time-bound.
- **Create Individual Development Plans**: Collaborate with each faculty member to create an individual development plan (IDP). Discuss their goals, aspirations, and areas for improvement. Identify the necessary resources, training programs, workshops, conferences, or other learning opportunities to help them achieve their goals.
- **Provide Resources and Support:** Allocate resources and support necessary for faculty development. This may include funding for attending conferences, access to relevant literature, subscriptions to academic journals, specialized software or equipment, and opportunities for collaboration or networking with peers.
- **Offer Training Programs**: Organize training programs tailored to the identified needs. These can include workshops, seminars, webinars, or online courses. Collaborate with internal or external experts to deliver training sessions on specific topics such as

pedagogy, assessment methods, curriculum development, research methodologies, grant writing, or educational technology.
- **Encourage Collaboration and Sharing:** Foster a culture of collaboration among faculty members. Please encourage them to share their expertise, best practices, and innovative teaching strategies. Create opportunities for peer mentoring, cross-disciplinary collaborations, and sharing of teaching materials and resources.
- **Support Research and Publication**: Support faculty members' research endeavors, such as research grants, research assistance, or dedicated research time. Please encourage them to publish their work in reputable journals or present at conferences to enhance their professional standing.
- **Mentorship and Coaching**: Establish mentorship programs where experienced faculty members can guide and support their colleagues. Encourage regular coaching sessions to address challenges, provide guidance, and facilitate professional growth. External coaching or mentoring opportunities can also be explored.
- **Evaluate and Monitor Progress**: Regularly assess and monitor the progress of faculty members in achieving their development goals. Provide feedback and support through periodic check-ins, performance evaluations, or self-assessment exercises. Adjust the development plan as needed to ensure continuous improvement.
- **Recognize and Celebrate Achievements**: Acknowledge and celebrate the achievements and milestones of faculty members. Recognize their growth, contributions, and successes. This can be

done through awards, public recognition, or sharing success stories within the institution.

Characteristics of an educational leader

Characteristics of an educational leader encompass a range of strategies, skills, traits, and beliefs that contribute to their effectiveness in leading educational institutions. Here are some key characteristics:

- **Visionary**: Educational leaders have a clear vision for the future of their institution and the ability to inspire others to work towards that vision.
- **Strong Communication Skills**: Effective leaders excel in communication, listening, and articulating ideas clearly. They foster open dialogue, actively engage with stakeholders, and effectively communicate their vision and expectations.
- **Adaptability**: Educational leaders embrace change and are flexible in their approach. They are willing to adapt strategies and practices to meet the evolving needs of students, staff, and the educational landscape.
- **Collaborative**: Leaders who value collaboration foster an environment of teamwork, trust, and shared decision-making. They actively seek stakeholder input, promote staff collaboration, and build partnerships with external organizations.
- **Instructional Leadership**: Educational leaders understand the importance of instructional quality and actively support and guide teachers in improving their instructional practices. They provide professional development opportunities, instructional resources, and feedback to enhance teaching and learning.

- **Problem-Solving Skills**: Effective leaders possess strong problem-solving skills and the ability to analyze complex issues, identify solutions, and make informed decisions. They approach challenges with a positive mindset and seek innovative solutions.
- **Emotional Intelligence**: Leaders with high emotional intelligence are self-aware, empathetic, and skilled in managing relationships. They understand the emotions and needs of others, build strong connections, and create a positive and supportive school culture.
- **Continuous Learner**: Educational leaders demonstrate a commitment to lifelong learning. They stay updated with the latest research, trends, and best practices in education and encourage a culture of professional growth and development among staff.
- **Ethical and Moral Integrity**: Leaders with strong ethical and moral integrity serve as role models for their community. They demonstrate honesty, fairness, and transparency in their actions and decision-making.
- **Student-Centered Focus**: Effective leaders place students at the center of their decision-making and prioritize their well-being, academic success, and personal growth. They advocate for equity, diversity, and inclusion, ensuring all students have access to high-quality education.

When combined with practical strategies, skills, traits, and beliefs, these characteristics enable educational leaders to create a positive and conducive learning environment, foster innovation, and drive student achievement and success.

In becoming an effective leader, incorporating the following principles into your approach can enhance your effectiveness, improve relationships, and achieve personal and professional success.

- BE PROACTIVE: Take charge of your actions by focusing on what you control and taking proactive steps to influence positive outcomes rather than being consumed by factors beyond your control.
- BEGIN WITH THE END IN MIND: Define your desired outcomes and create a clear roadmap. Set specific goals and establish a plan that aligns with your long-term vision.
- PUT FIRST THINGS: Prioritize your tasks and responsibilities based on importance rather than urgency. By focusing on your most important goals and tasks, you can avoid getting caught up in a cycle of constantly reacting to immediate demands.
- THINK WIN-WIN: Foster collaborative relationships by seeking mutually beneficial solutions. Instead of adopting a win-lose mentality, strive for outcomes that satisfy all parties involved, promoting trust and long-term cooperation.
- SEEK FIRST TO UNDERSTAND, THEN TO BE UNDERSTOOD: Develop practical communication skills by actively listening and empathizing with others. You can build rapport and influence them more effectively by genuinely understanding their needs, concerns, and perspectives.
- SYNERGIZE: Encourage synergy by embracing diversity and leveraging individuals' or teams' unique strengths and perspectives. By fostering collaboration and creative problem-solving, you can generate innovative solutions that satisfy the needs of all stakeholders.

- SHARPEN THE SAW: Prioritize self-care and personal growth by engaging in activities that renew and rejuvenate you mentally, physically, spiritually, and emotionally. Investing time in your well-being can increase motivation and energy levels and achieve a healthy work-life balance.

Productivity

You feel overwhelmed as you sit on your disk with home problems and work chores like emails, meetings, texts, teaching materials, and student feedback, bringing your multitasking abilities into hellish nightmares. Your phone rings and your supervisor reminds you of the expected report due in one hour. You start to breathe heavily, and your heart races as you hate to disappoint anyone feeling your Reputation is on the line.

Deep in your heart, you believe you have become an average kind of faculty; how did I get to this point? You ask yourself; I used to be the best.

I want to tell you, you are not alone in this boat. Life, as we know it, has changed, and much is expected of us. I remember walking down the corridor of my division, thriving with people talking to each other and ideas exchanges while collaborating, using each other as resources for productive means. As I visited the same corridor a month ago, silence hit me like a ghost town lightning. All faculty doors closed, and every Professor minded their own business. The makeup of the new division of old and new faculty was uncultured and needed unification of a productive environment.

This reality is not the story of a particular college but most community colleges. Revitalizing the division mind needs a drastic compiling makeover, giving birth or restoration to a productive, diverse equitable faculty to bring life to the masses with advanced economic growth to a new thriving community.

We have been paralyzed by information overload with exceeding outcome expectations. Covid19 has tested and shocked us completely. We find ourselves alone, and our human presence is wanted. No one to talk to face to face; the digital world failed us as preparation for its efficiency was lacking.

Community colleges have opened their doors to their students, but many have given up on their dreams. Receiving government income while staying at home has become the norm. Our duty as faculty is to shake our community and wake them up from their sleep. But it starts with us; we must be revived and restored with new visions for our personal lives and society.

Current and new leadership nationwide must cultivate higher education's revival one institution at a time. Our curriculum needs our attention as the needs of our society and workforce partners are changing.

As faculty, our work expectations require us to be organized and productive. We need to learn how to unplug ourselves from unnecessary activities, pause and reflect on our need for each other and our research capabilities, and analytically create ways to be productive and valuable to our division environment.

It stands to reason to be productive and find a way to reduce the surge of digital distractions. There are three types of people in this world: those who make things happen, those who watch things happen, and those who wonder what happened. So, what kind of people do you belong to in Higher Education?

If you are like me, you are the kind of person that makes things happen; otherwise, you need to check your reason for being in education. We need to stop reacting and start responding by being productive in our daily actions and duties, thinking about the division as a whole, and denying self-deception, self-glorification, and self-centeredness.

We will tackle complex challenges and turn our curiosities into meaningful goals. Breaking our goals into smaller and more manageable events and then taking action, weeding out distractions so we can focus our time and energy on what matters.

Intentional Mindfulness

We live in an age where technology offers limitless possibilities to occupy ourselves, yet we are left feeling empty, distracted, unproductive, and disconnected from what is essential.

> *To successfully navigate the world around us,*
> *We must learn how to navigate ourselves*
> *inwardly.*

Being mindful requires us to be fully awake from our slumber and aware of where we are, who we are, why we are, and what we want. If you are unorganized, it's time you become one. Do you remember hearing a quote or a speech that deeply touched you and changed your life? Wisdom inspired you and gave you purpose, walking through the narrow door and leaving the wide gate behind with its chaos.

"Intentional living is the art of making our own choices before others' choices make us." Richie Norton.

Decluttering our mind

William Morris said, "Have nothing in your home that you do not know to be useful or believe to be beautiful." The mind produces between 50K to 70K thoughts daily, generating enough content to make a book. But the book's content is ambiguously coherent, and the thoughts are not neatly composed. We become what we call busy; our minds are challenged with so many issues simultaneously, spreading our focus so thin that nothing gets the attention it needs.

> *For most of us, "being busy" is code for*
> *being functionally overwhelmed*

We do not perform greatness because we work on many things simultaneously, producing average work. We sit at our desks, and we ask ourselves should text type, call, email, swipe, pin, tweet, skype, facetime, Zoom, or message. We must update, upgrade, reboot, log in, authenticate, reset our password, clear our cookies, empty our cache, and sacrifice our firstborn before we can get where we are going.

Where do I start? We need to simplify our work and not take too much work simultaneously. We must reduce the number of choices to save time and increase productivity. The more decisions we must make, the harder it becomes to make them well. We become overwhelmed, so we try to treat our symptoms with more distractions; drinking, eating, traveling, and watching tv, we become more tired and stressed.

> *We need to reduce the number of decisions we*
> *burden ourselves*
> *with so we can focus on what matters.*

Leadership Development Pressures

Life has two valuable and mindful resources: our time and energy. Investing in these resources will help us identify and focus on what is meaningful by stripping away what is meaningless and accomplishing more by working less.

Time Management: Management of time does not exist. Twenty-four hours a day will never change; we can not bend it. Therefore, time management is managing ourselves by intentionally structuring our schedule to serve our goals best. Living out our priorities and achieving our goals requires being intentional and disciplined. It requires strategically organizing tasks to maximize productivity.

> ***Until we can manage time, we can manage nothing else.***
> *Peter F. Drucker*
>
> ***Time is irreplaceable***

What is the point of rushing only to arrive at the wrong destination? A lack of clear purpose, vague goals, and diffusion of effort lead to either quick progress toward a meaningless destination or slower progress toward the goal that matters. Defending our precious time, energy, and resources is the first step.

Energy Protection: Our energy is our currency; we need to spend it well by becoming more aware of what is worth our energy. We need to learn how to use our energy wisely in the most important and impactful ways to make a difference.

We will always face a moment of complexity in our work life, which makes our workday challenging and stressful. Feeling overwhelmed at work typically means experiencing stress due to the amount or difficulty of the work that our job requires us to complete. We may be working to overcome the challenge of participating in complex projects or having numerous tasks with tight deadlines. There are ways we can reduce or eliminate this overwhelming feeling, such as taking plenty of breaks, asking for help, or telling our supervisor when our workload feels too heavy.

Here are five ways to use our energy correctly:

- **Notice our energy.** Where do we spend it? We see things differently when we look at life with an energy lens. We set our phone to beep at random times during the day as a prompt to notice how I'm spending my energy at that moment — both visibly (doing) and invisibly (thinking). Simply doing this little energy check-in began to change our habits.
- **Know what matters to us** by:
    - Create a to-do list.
    - Build and follow a schedule.
    - Ask for guidance when needed.
    - Express our thoughts or concerns to team members.
    - Receive feedback on our work.
    - Be honest about our workload.
    - Maintain a healthy work-life balance.
- **Plan wise energy investment.** Once we know which things matter most to us, schedule as many of them into our life as possible. Please put them on our calendar. Let them force out activities that represent energy leaks. Where do we want to spend our

mental energy? We find that perseverating over things (or people) that annoy us is rarely a valuable way to consume energy. But thinking about what we can learn from something almost always is. Let our learning mind "force out" our complaining mind. Scheduling time to glean insights at the end of the day can be incredibly valuable.

- **Most importantly, plan where not to invest**. Once we notice our energy, we will see things we do and ways we think that are pointless energy drains. While it's surprisingly hard to stop doing something midstream, it's much less painful not to start in the first place. Don't enter a conversation that we know will rile us up and get us nowhere.
- **Finally, don't spend much time thinking about this**. We don't have to get it right. Optimizing our energy expenditure can be its counterproductive energy drain, like Pulling ourselves out of one useless conversation, stopping ourselves from responding to one silly email, letting go of one nagging thought, and you'll be a more intelligent investor of your energy.

What is leadership competency?

Leadership competencies are leadership skills and behaviors that contribute to superior performance. Organizations can better identify and develop their next generation of leaders by using a competency-based approach to leadership. (Brownwell, 2006)

Focusing on leadership competencies and skill development promotes better Leadership (Mumford, 2007). Organizations can use a competency approach to determine the positions requiring specific competencies. Competency is not gained by knowing how to do everything but by knowing the task and how to accomplish it. All competencies have indicators, that allows them to be observed and measured. A leadership competency model is a group of competencies linked to leadership excellence in a specific organization (Harris, 2020).

All leaders must learn and develop the necessary competencies that evoke their abilities for effective and superior performance results. Influential leaders need technical expertise fundamental to a particular job and the leadership competencies applicable to the leadership level of the position. A leadership competency model validates the organization's vision and strategy by providing a framework by which the the educational institutions can select, develop, and evaluate their leaders.

A competency model is a collection of competencies defining successful performance in a particular work setting—there are several ways of creating an organizational leadership competency model.

1. The first method is conducting interviews with the different levels of leaders in the educational institute to understand what specific skills, abilities, and knowledge sets are important for their success and the success of their department. After the data is collected, analyzed into a competency model.
2. The second method is to organize a leadership meeting and discuss the organization's climate, culture, and strategy. The outcome of this discussion would give birth to Competencies in support of the organization.
3. The third method is to select a set from a list of known leadership competencies related to organizational success, reflecting on the experience and industry best practices as a guide.

When completing a list of competencies, they must be defined in a non-complex language to understand the employees. The definition needs to specify the what and why.

Develop Leadership Competencies?

Developing leadership competencies is a continuous process that requires self-reflection, learning, and practice. Here are some steps you can take to develop your leadership competencies:

- **Define your leadership vision**: Clarify your values, beliefs, and vision for leadership. Consider what kind of leader you aspire to be and the impact you want to have on others and the organization.
- **Identify your strengths and areas for improvement**: Reflect on your current leadership skills and abilities. Identify your strengths that you can leverage and areas where you can improve. Seek feedback from others to gain different perspectives on your leadership style.
- **Continuous learning**: Stay curious and committed to learning. Read books, attend seminars, and participate in workshops or training programs focused on leadership development. Stay updated with the latest research and best practices in leadership.
- **Seek mentorship and coaching**: Find mentors or coaches who can guide you and provide valuable insights. They can help you identify blind spots, challenge assumptions, and develop specific leadership competencies.
- **Practice self-awareness**: Cultivate self-awareness by reflecting on your thoughts, emotions, and actions as a leader. Understand

how your behavior impacts others and how you can adapt your leadership style to different situations and individuals.
- **Develop practical communication skills**: Communication is crucial for leadership. Enhance your ability to listen actively, articulate your ideas clearly, and provide constructive feedback. Practice both verbal and written communication skills to convey your messages effectively.
- **Build strong relationships**: Develop your interpersonal skills to build strong relationships with your team members, colleagues, and stakeholders—Foster trust, empathy, and collaboration. Seek to understand others' perspectives and create a supportive environment.
- **Develop decision-making and problem-solving skills**: Leaders often face complex decisions and challenges. Enhance your ability to analyze situations, weigh options, and make informed decisions. Develop problem-solving skills to address issues effectively and find innovative solutions.
- **Embrace adaptability and resilience**: Leadership requires navigating change and uncertainty. Cultivate adaptability and resilience to handle challenges and setbacks. Be open to new ideas and approaches, and learn from failures or mistakes.
- **Practice leadership in various contexts**: Seek opportunities to lead, whether within your current role, volunteering, or taking on new projects. Practice applying your leadership skills and competencies in different situations, and learn from each experience.

Criteria for Practical Competency Model?

While having competencies for your leaders is crucial, not all competencies are created alike. How can you tell a robust competency model from a weak one? There are three critical criteria when building your competency model for leaders (Development Dimensions International, Inc., 2020).

- Align to strategic business priorities.
- Differentiate for leader levels.
- Focus on observable behaviors.

Leadership time implication

- leaders must prepare to make the most of their time daily by developing foundational leadership skills (such as effective communication, coaching, managing work, and performance).
- Begin with the end in mind. Learn the institution's short and long-term strategic and cultural priorities and the portfolio of skills, knowledge, experience, and attributes to set the leaders up for success.
- Take a pipeline approach. Implement and ongoing development of skills throughout the year. Your organization's leadership is only as strong as its weakest link.
- Continue initiatives to identify leadership potential early, plan for future leadership needs, and provide growth opportunities. Build and maintain a culture that promotes growth and engagement so institutions can retain talented leaders and address their desire for fulfilling careers.

Leadership is a relationship between those who aspire to lead and those who choose or are required to follow. Understanding and interacting with others is critically important in Higher education settings. Higher education institutions are generally organized and governed according to two outwardly contradictory practices—hierarchical and individualistic. The most effective academic leaders know that developing and enduring positive working relationships is the only way to achieve significant change through developing and sustaining positive working relationships (Kouzes & Posner, 2019).

Knowing people, and having trusting relationships with them, is just as fundamental as knowing information. Even in this nanosecond world of e-everything, this conclusion is consistent with the facts. According to the World Economic Forum's report, The Future of Jobs, strong social and collaboration skills will be in higher demand than spectacular technical ones (World Economic Forum, 2016). It's not the web of technology that matters the most; it's the web of people. Social capital, the network of relationships among people, joins intellectual and financial.

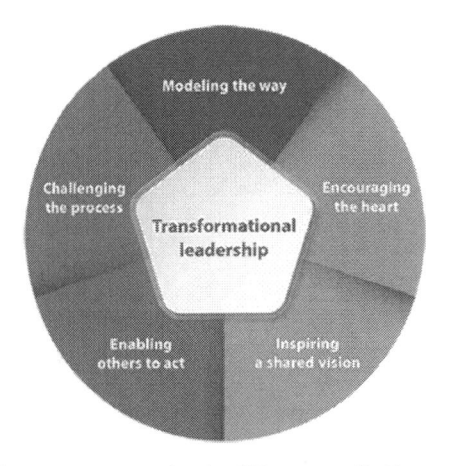

Success in Transformational Leadership and success in life has been and will continue to be, a function of how well people work with one another. Success in leading will be wholly dependent on the capacity to build and sustain those human relationships that enable people to make extraordinary things happen regularly (Kouzes & Posner, 2019).

To build a truly effective relationship, we must follow the following practices.

- **Model the way**. It is our behavior that wins our respect. First, we must be clear about our guiding principles before holding them up for others. Once we know the core values, we can give them a voice, share them with others, and act on them.
    - As Leaders, we must also ensure that what we do is consistent with our values and standards. As leaders, we need to walk the talk. Our deeds are far more important than our words when demonstrating our seriousness about what we say.
- **Inspire a shared vision.** As leaders, we need to live our lives backward. See the idea as a picture; much like an architect drawing blueprints, The clear image of the future moves us forward. Be like the GPS; when deciding on the destination and knowing the current place, see the best route to keep the focus on the goal while executing the objectives. People will not follow until they accept the vision as their own.
- **Challenge the process**; be willing to step out into the unknown, innovate, grow, and improve.
- **Enable others to act**; Leadership is a team effort to make extraordinary things happen. Foster collaboration, develop relationships and build trust. Work is to make people feel strong, capable, and committed.
- **Encourage the heart**; It is your part to show appreciation for people's contributions and create a celebration culture. Four characteristics of emotional intelligence are vital in building your leadership relationship competency (Modern Psychology

Publishing, 2019). The four are Self-awareness, Social Awareness, Relationship management, and Self-regulation or self-control.

Identify your strength and weaknesses, your beliefs, emotions, and motivations. Self-awareness is the ability to understand and be aware of one's personality. It requires a high level of honesty in dealing with self-assessment. For this reason, many leaders are self-deceived because of the intuitive nature of this skill.

Transformational Leadership

Transformational leadership is an approach that initiates a change in individuals' and systems' lives. It creates a valuable difference in the individual with the end product in mind, developing and producing leaders authentically integrated with motivational morals.

Becoming a leader hoping to transform others is a noble and powerful change tool. In Jesus's words, you have to be born again. I am not speaking in religious terms but in human reality. Being transformed is not a skill you learn or an act you put on; it is like the metamorphosis of a caterpillar into a butterfly. To become a transformational leader, you must become well-rounded in three fundamental areas.

- Become a leader worth following; your people will follow as they see your leadership presence.
- Build leaders worth following; organizations need stronger leaders to sustain and grow.
- Lead organizations people want to join. People desire to attach their names to a thriving lead organization.

Do you want to help others climb beyond what they believed possible to the higher levels? Such events will happen through transformation, and, like metamorphosis, transformation requires your guidance if people experience a dramatic change in their life. The secret to significant transformation happened through three primary elements:

- **Restoration**: Restoration of people to whom they are by helping them understand their temperament.
- **Taking Out**: Leaders must stop doing certain things to become their best selves, which is the most challenging element.
- **Raising**: We remind people who they can be, fighting for their highest leadership level.

The range of leadership introduces four elements of transformational leadership:

- **Individualized Consideration** – Transformational leadership involves offering support and encouragement to individual followers. To foster supportive relationships, transformational leaders keep lines of communication open so that followers feel free to share ideas and that leaders can immediately recognize each follower's unique contributions.

- **Intellectual Stimulation** – Transformational leaders not only challenge the status quo; they also encourage creativity among followers. The leader encourages followers to explore new ways of doing things and learning opportunities.

- **Inspirational motivation** – Transformational leaders have a clear vision to articulate to followers. These leaders can also help followers experience the same passion and motivation to fulfill these goals.

- **Idealized Influence** –The transformational leader serves as a role model for followers. Because followers trust and respect the leader, they emulate this individual and internalize their ideals.

Leadership Competencies

Adaptability
Flexibility, change, and fresh ideas

Integrity
Leading with character, courage and consistency at all time

Discipline
Meeting complex demand, team agility

Accountability
Demonstrate personal accountability, ownership, results, and consequences

Organizational Awareness
Understanding the tangible and intangible data

Authenticity
Leading with moral values, truthfulness, openness, and positivity

Innovation
Leading with constant improvement

Compassion
Leading through communication, social awareness and relational intelligence

Conflict Management
Listening and problem solving to remove colflict

Inspiration
Motivating, encouraging, and influencing others

Wisdom
Today's decision making will impact tomorrow

Vision
Developing clear mission and purpose

Leadership Competency Development

Leadership Competencies

Before we dive into leadership competencies, an awareness of a particular competency that lies beneath all competencies can influence the lives of our students and employees of all levels. Ignoring such competency can harm leadership function and higher education enrollment and retention.

When Latinos became the largest ethnic group in California, it was headline-making news. While fairly old news (data from 2012), higher education is painfully shown in realizing that the student population looks significantly different than it did ten years ago.

The writer is an Israeli-Christian Arab who is a citizen of the U.S. In Israel, driving between two villages is like flying to a different country; even though they speak the same language, their culture is entirely different, and acting in the same manner, can be life endangerment (You can lose your life). Last weekend as my wife and I were shopping in Houston, Texas, we experienced the same. The world as we know it has changed dramatically.

Cultural competence is having and applying knowledge and skill in four areas: awareness of one's cultural worldview; recognition of one's attitudes toward cultural differences; realization of different cultural practices and worldviews; and thoughtfulness in cross-cultural. Our focus is competency development.

Competency 1 - Integrity

Integrity is the core foundation upon which we build all leadership competencies. Many leaders think they are beyond reach and above reproach. Suppose we attempt to build our house on the sinking sand of deceit, cheating, and stealing. In that case, we might get trapped in muddling situations where our Reputation will be destroyed or even deal with criminal problems. We decide to contravene our moral code and the concepts of truth and honesty. We may rationalize the decision as unimportant and never be noticed (Schirmer, 2021).

Integrity has no middle ground; you are described as trustworthy or untrustworthy, honest or dishonest, incorruptible or correctable. When we decide to compromise our integrity in a small way and discover that, at this time, it has no consequence; we will believe it is satisfactory to repeat the process. We betray our self which leads to self-deception. Therefore such Action leads to a loss of trust and destroys relationships.

Leadership is impossible without integrity, and integrity is inconceivable without trust. Integrity is not the absence of deceit and falsehood but the embodiment of truth. Trust-based integrity leadership delivers personal, institutional, societal, and systemic purpose-driven, value-enhancing positive impacts.

Leading with integrity

"The supreme quality for leadership is unquestionably integrity. Without it, no real success is possible, no matter whether it is on a section gang, a football field, in an army, or in an office."
-Dwight D. Eisenhower

At its core, the current concept of integrity is the combination of consistency in words and actions and adherence to morality and one's values in these actions.

The Elements of Integrity

Integrity, an essential quality of successful leadership, has taken many forms—the five main elements of leadership integrity and what they mean to you as a leader.

1. **Wholeness**. Integrity includes a leader's values, daily actions, and primary organizational aims.
2. **Consistency between words and actions**. A demonstrated consistency concerning social behavior.
3. **Consistency in the face of adversity**. It is consistency in the face of temptation and challenge.
4. **Being true to oneself**. Conceptualized as acting according to one's conscience.
5. **Morality/Ethics**. Acting by socially acceptable behavior, such as honesty, trustworthiness, justice, and compassion

Practice makes perfect

In leadership, you make decisions in seconds and are expected to act consistently with integrity every time, which can prove very difficult. Just as professional basketball players practice their free throws to develop the muscle memory to make the shot in the big game, you too can build your moral muscle memory (Gentile, 2010) for acting with integrity.

Ask yourself these questions?

- What if you knew what you believed was right?
- How would you get it done?
- What would you say, to whom, and in what sequence?

- What information and analysis would you need to build a case? What allies could you find or develop to depend upon?

Act on what you can do, not what you should not do. Quote to remember and live by:

Bob Macdonald, Retired Chairman, President, and CEO, of P&G
"You must live by your word and actions and know that is the most powerful demonstration of leadership."

Paul Polman, Chief Executive Officer, Unilever
"Successful Leadership requires a high level of integrity and trust, today more than ever. This is true for us individually, but also how we work together as teams."

Competency 2 - Accountability

Accountability is expressed through Action, not through words. It is "doing what you said you'd do, when and how you said you'd do it." David Cottrell, it is not what happened to us but how we choose to respond that determines our plans, actions, and relationships (Schirmer, 2021).

"Accountability is like an invisible constraint placed around a leader's ability to operate and control" (Harris, 2020). Accountability is a mindset, a way of thinking where results matter and the leader is personally invested in the outcome that he is responsible for and leaders take this very seriously.

Accountability has the potential to boost your entire team's performance. A winning team is distinguished from an average or failing by making yourself and others. Being personally responsible and ensuring others are accountable is an essential policy that leaders should implement to drive successful results. Accountability starts with you. Don't try to shift blame away from yourself by delegating accountability. Leaders who are held accountable take responsibility, address problems, and develop procedures to prevent future blunders (Schirmer, 2021).

A leader's ultimate responsibility is for their behavior, results, and the outcomes of others working for them. A leader holds the mirror up first and examines their shortcomings before they seek to explore those of others. If the leader underachieves, their immediate supervisor will look at their failings and theirs alone.

This core qualification involves the ability to meet organizational goals and expectations. This executive core qualification is the ability to make decisions that produce high-quality results by applying technical knowledge, analyzing problems, and calculating risks. Holds self and others accountable for measurable high-quality, timely, and cost-effective results. Determines objectives sets priorities, and delegates work. Accepts responsibility for mistakes and complies with established control systems and rules.

Feedback in accountability is essential, especially when it stings; it intends to care for our well-being. It aims to help the leader improve and accomplish future outcomes through positive performance instruction.

Clear accountability language.

- No matter what outcome you are working to create, make sure everyone involved has the same mental "picture" of the desired end state.
- Have you ever been in the middle of a conversation and found that you and the other person are talking about two different things? That's because the meanings of words are in people's minds, not dictionaries. People have definitions for words like "plan" or "best." Differently than you. Be as specific and define your words as possible.
- If you are like most leaders, you've seen a repeated occurrent problem, but no one ever sounds the alarm. Be the voice your organization needs. Be willing to proclaim that something needs to change to increase accountability.
- Do you get stressed over unrealistic deadlines? No need to create stress by inflicting self-imposed, unreasonable time and date requirements. Do your part to keep time and dates realistic.

- Clarify the date, time, and time zone in all communications. Adding a simple CDT (Central Daylight Time), or whatever time zone you refer to, is a good habit.
- The leader will be more accessible when everyone understands the requirements for establishing accountability.
    - **C**ulture: How I inspire and encourage communication with others
    - **L**anguage: What I say to generate shared understanding
    - **E**xpectations: How I describe the results
    - **A**bility: How I ensure the skills, knowledge, and resources are available
    - **R**eward and consequences: What we will gain or risk
- Determining the best owner is vital for projects. The most technically qualified person may not always be the best for ownership. Typically the best owner has excellent project management skills and is enthusiastic about the project. A passionate person who is less qualified may work harder and be more successful, especially in inspiring others to soar.
- Quantify the outcomes and avoid unmeasurable words like "better."
- Clear expectations mean enough communication occurs; consequently, no questions are unanswered at the end of every contact.
- Determine if your team is lacking; discover the reasons and if some are related to a lack of accountability, such as changing (or conflicting) priorities, unclear expectations, a lack of ownership, absence of consequences, unclear roles or responsibilities, lack of

collaboration, or lack of transparency. Create a list to help you understand what you might do (Evans & Biech, 2018).

As you move toward mastering accountability:

- You will offer realistic promises and hit your deadlines.
- You will be clear about your priorities, scheduling your time accordingly.
- You will value the people you work with— they can feel it and feel the same about you.
- Your meetings will be more productive, and,
- You will lead the organizational change— where your enthusiasm is contagious, no matter where you sit on the org chart (Evans & Biech, 2018).

Thoughts to remember: Little things matter, Disrupt normal, Keep it real, Be vulnerable, Develop yourself, Listen without defending, speak without offending, Express appreciation, and Revisit your work.

Competency 3 - Authenticity

In my role in higher education, I meet many leaders who are great actors. Leaders like these are confused and shocked when employees can not wait to stop working for them. They are only interested in you when needed, dropping you like a dead fly afterward. Authentic leadership is the healthy matching internal **values** and beliefs with exterior behavior. Authentic leadership identifies the **uniqueness** and leadership style and establishes decisions that embody your personality and **morals** (Gaddam, 2021).

Authentic leadership is about leading from the essence of our being to inspire others to contribute toward fulfilling a shared mission. Authentic leadership is at the heart of cultures of incredible innovation, commitment, outstanding experience, and development. Therefore, when leaders bring their authentic selves to work, they inspire motivated, creative, engaged followers who participate enthusiastically.

Authentic leaders lead with their hearts and mind. They have an approach to truthfulness, openness, and positivity, choosing their words carefully and knowing their words have an impact.

Authentic leadership inspires trust and motivation. Through courageous actions, authentic leaders alleviate fears for their followers, encourage them to take bold steps, and make them believe in the worthiness of a mission. Curbing from the consistent, constant, and build confidence and motivate followers.

How do you develop authenticity?

Leaders must communicate effectively to build trust and demonstrate sincerity. It's essential to have clarity of thinking and message, so consider, learn, and maintain what you want to express. Every question and every interaction is an opportunity to communicate one's thoughts, ideals, and vision. But, in any relation, maintain a balance between oversharing and under-sharing.

Warmth is an effective way to interact, communicate and relate. Using words like "we" and "us" increase inclusion and inspires listeners. Show warmth. Smile while you interact. There is a warmth in you; you must tap into it and express it by smiling but do not act. They will see through you very quickly. It will become a disaster.

Include trusted colleagues and friends in your strategy for added authenticity. They can act as sounding boards, provide feedback, be cheerleaders, and solve problems. However, you must stay steadfast and believe your instincts when it says what is best for you. Without a dedication to a minor, daily modifications over time, you're unlikely to make genuine, long-term progress.

Evaluate your objectives. You can better understand how linked your activities are with your values once you've identified your likes and dislikes. Examine what you've already given up and be clear about what's essential to you and what you'll and won't do to get there. Remember that there are no "right" trade-offs to make, and your preferences will likely vary. Every exchange you make might not seem "RIGHT," as your favor might change over time.

What are your core principles? Understanding what you care about most is an essential part of acting truthfully. Although this may appear straightforward, we frequently overlook determining what is necessary.

Your leadership challenge should be sincere and demand growth and new information. Consider the difference and noticeable dissimilarities between the image you want to give off or portray and the picture others have of you. The rigid feeling of maintaining a specific picture is a significant block and a hindrance to authenticity. An encompassing understanding of your present image and leadership brand can go a long way. However, before making any modifications, take a good, accurate snapshot of your current image. Give time or create one to note and see what others think of you and their reasons.

Competency 4 – Compassion

Genuinely seeking to understand and respect others' perspectives and emotions, encouraging a culture of compassion, empathy, and support within and beyond the organization. Compassion has become a fundamental characteristic of leadership and a crucial leadership skill.

Compassion is a core necessity for building and maintaining solid relationships with others; where it is lacking, it stands out as a negative. Basic human decency entails showing compassion for others when required, and employees are sensitive to how their leaders deal with their welfare and misfortunes. The ability to demonstrate care, kindness, and concern for the welfare of others is not only a desirable human quality but also a trait that develops leadership effectiveness. Self-compassion motivates leaders to grow out of their weaknesses, correct their transgressions, and learn-grow from failure.

Emotions provide vital data to us; it is not essentially good or bad but a fundamental unit of information. We always forget critical information about us humans, we are full of emotion, and often we operate from such a base. When compassionate towards our subordinates, we deal with the whole person, full of emotions like Intense anxiety, depression, anger, guilt, and other painful emotional disorders. Do you remember a time in your life when you operated from such places? How was it for you? Was it productive? Or did it introduce an emotionally stormy environment? Whenever people have problems hard to solve to their satisfaction, they tend to get angry, resulting in hostility directed at employees or upper leaders.

A compassionate leader can bring understanding, appreciation, and healing to most employees by using particular heartfelt phrases to calm the storm in the heart and minds of the employees.

The compassionate workplace is one where (Hargreaves, 2021):

- Compassion is a guiding principle and underpinning value and is recognizable through its members' culture, inforcing language, values, actions, and behaviors.

- Leaders and their teams prioritize relationships, connectivity, collaboration, cooperation, and co-creation.
- Leaders are highly competent managers with solid management and business skills enhanced by compassionate principles and approaches.
- Organizational structures are configured to empower, enable, and support their members.
- Hierarchy is flattened at every opportunity, minimizing control and enhancing support, and autonomy is a reality for everyone.
- Inclusion takes center stage – the focus is on ensuring that people feel they belong rather than merely fit in.
- Reward, recognize, and celebrate.
- Simplify, and inspire values and behaviors.
- Leaders focus on engaging with others through building relationships, connectivity, and communication and helping others succeed.
- Learning and improvement focus on everyone.
- A vibrant culture is awakened and not suppressed.
- People experience a compassionate workplace community where they can thrive and create value.

Competency 5 – Wisdom

Many leaders have a significant amount of knowledge and intellect. However, possessing these assets is not sufficient for making the correct decision. Gaudiani (1998) describes wisdom as the available store of thought, collected over thousands of years, that calls for living in ways that sustain the well-being of others. Wisdom guides leaders toward what they should do and who they should be. Wisdom can include characteristics such as the ability of the leader to judge facts morally and decisively and the power to frame questions and answers.

When examining leadership wisdom, I determined that wisdom is not one competence but a multi-dimensional structure of ordinary ways of being, living, and dealings. Wisdom involves seeing things as they are. Acting in prudent and effective ways, working with the well-being of the whole in mind, knowing when to act and when not to, being able to handle whatever arises with peace of mind, having an effective, compassionate, holistic response, and being able to anticipate potential problems and avoid them.

Wise leaders live their daily lives following thoughtful perspectives and wise values. Their actions make the world around them a better place. Therefore, they resolve conflicts and so maximize harmony and general well-being. Wisdom is the ability to make sound choices and good decisions. It is intelligence shaped by experience.

Meeker (2004) sums wisdom up as a state of the human mind characterized by profound understanding and deep insight. Wisdom is a perception of the relativity and relationships among things wherever it exists. It is often, but not necessarily, accompanied by extensive formal knowledge. Unschooled people can acquire wisdom; wise people are found among carpenters, fishermen, and homemakers.

Many criteria could be used to judge whether or not decisions are wise. Kane suggests that wise decisions are more likely to emanate from consultative decision-making as wise decision-making involves deep and equal consideration of a range of perspectives. Wisdom can only happen in circumstances that are ethical and social. Kane (2003) holds that wise leaders look at things clearly and do not allow their judgment to be overshadowed by their own personal biases. They base their decisions and actions on the truth.

Competency 6 – Inspiration

Inspirational Leadership competency is the ability to inspire and guide people to do the job and bring out their best. With inspiration, you can articulate a shared mission that motivates and offers a common purpose beyond people's day-to-day tasks. To inspire, a leader must be strong in E.I. competencies, including emotional self-awareness, self-control, positive outlook, organizational awareness, influence, and teamwork.

Motivate others to achieve organizational goals. Act as a role model.

Key Behaviors

- Demonstrates integrity and fairness.
- Inspires others' commitment to their work and organizational goals.
- Helps others see the benefits of doing their job well, for themselves, their Students, and the greater good.
- Upholds the highest standards of scientific research and business practices.
- Acts as a role model.
- Recognizes the contributions of others.
- Champions innovation and creativity by encouraging, recognizing, and rewarding those who take the initiative, develop new ideas or concepts or improve work processes or methods.
- Actively embraces diversity by creating, leading, and managing an inclusive workplace that maximizes each person's talents.

Competency 7 – Vision

Vision is the umbrella of any educational department's values, beliefs, and goals. Its strategies evolve, giving birth to a new reality. Leaders should not lose sight of the vision because of everyday battles caused by change but refocus and reconsider their tactics, visualize their outcome, and execute accurately, making their vision a reality.

Communicate the vision through multiple channels. The vision is not communicated enough to stay present and familiar to faculty and staff. Every leader must own the responsibility of communicating the vision. Having the vision shared from various channels increases its embrace substantially.

Make sure that you (the leader) and your team always know which direction you are pursuing. While sharing the vision, execute the following process:

- Educate, and act as your team instructor. State, explain, discuss, assess, and verify their understanding and consequences. Please do not assume they know what is on paper or your mind.
- Demonstrate, and show the team how it works by increasing the knowledge and understanding of the vision.
- Facilitate; let your team show you their competence.
- Trust but verify. Allow the team to work on the vision but verify its execution.

Competency 8 – Conflict management

Conflict management encourages creative tension and differences of opinion. Anticipates and takes steps to prevent counterproductive confrontations. Manages and constructively resolves conflicts and disagreements.

Conflict is a disagreement through which the parties involved perceive a threat to their needs, interests, or concerns; despite their first attempts at agreement, they do not yet understand a course of Action, usually because their values, perspectives, and opinions are contradictory.

Conflict is avoidable but often needs to:

- It benefits to raise and address problems.
- Energizes work to be focused on the most critical priorities.
- It helps people "be real" and motivates them to participate fully
- It helps people learn how to recognize and benefit from their differences.

Conflicts can be divided into two main types, which are:

- **Affective conflict** deals with interpersonal relationships or incompatibilities not directly related to achieving the group's responsibilities, often driven by emotion and perceptions about somebody else's motives and character
- **Substantive conflict** involves disagreements among group members about the content of performed task or the performance itself. This type of conflict occurs when two or more social entities disagree on recognizing and solving a task problem, including differences in viewpoints, ideas, and opinions.

We have three broad choices when we are facing conflict:

- We can choose to discuss and debate our differences, respecting each other's opinion
- We can argue about these differences, i.e., we are convinced we are right and the other should have our perspective.

- We can create conflict about these differences by imposing our way of doing things.

Understanding that we have different personalities, conflict occurs when we give in to fulfilling the needs of our temperament. Humility is needed in any dispute when a requirement has been discussed, and an understanding of each other's positions is shown.

As denying people's needs causes conflict, the successful resolution must involve satisfying those needs; otherwise, the conflict could simmer and re-ignite. If you want a lasting win, look for success for the other. It does not have to be win-lose; this win-lose mindset forces us to be competitive. This mindset is appropriate in sports but can miss the point where people are concerned. The win-lose tactic assumes there is not enough for everyone to have what they need. Using the correct phrases helps in many ways; for example, 'I would like to find a solution that works for both of us.' 'How do you suggest we go about this?'

Win-win is more to be expected when people

- focus on both sets of needs, concerns, and feelings,
- Respect each other's views,
- See the issue as a mutual problem to be solved,
- Are prepared to listen and compromise?
- Are not interested in winning at any cost,
- opt for power *with* rather than power *over*.

A four-step model is helpful to use in conflict management in an organization.

1. Attend to the other person first.
2. Explore the need behind the want for all sides.

3. Invite the other's solutions.
4. Build maximum win-win.

Steps one and two show that we are trying to understand the other person. Steps three and four show that we are willing to meet their needs

Many conflicts arise simply because we assume others and our interpretations of the things said. Such disputes could be defused by a few minutes of skillful and honest discussion. In our conversation, we must stay current, think of solutions, and imagine ourselves in the other person's shoes.

The more people involved in a conflict, the more complex it will be to meet everyone's needs. We must consider their wants, concerns, and feelings to understand their needs. That will bring forth possible solutions which would bring an agreed solution.

Problem-solving

"Most of our problems occur because we act without thinking or keep thinking without acting" ZZig Ziglar.

Problem-solving is an everyday occurrence in the workplace. Sometimes it is a formal problem-solving, but most often, it is done during small snatches of conversation between managers and workers while standing in the hall or leaning on a desk or wall support and during coffee breaks and lunch hours.

Problem-Solving has one goal: to produce a solution that fulfills the institution's vision, goals, and values. Many employees forget the job description that explains their duties and commitment to their institute's vision, goals, values, and strategic plans. All employees needed to be reminded of such a fact regularly. Their agenda must be defeated and annulled so the institutional living organism can survive.

The benefit of problem-solving

- Minimize recurring problems
- Improve operational efficiency
- Provide a repeatable approach
- Promote team collaboration
- Enable critical decision making
- Create visibility of a problem
- Discover the root cause of a problem
- Identify improvement opportunities

Skills needed and demonstrated with efficient Problem-Solving. Many people struggle to successfully resolve problems at work and in their personal life because they lack specific skills such as:

- Observation
- Listening
- Empathy
- Patience
- Persistence
- Respect for others
- Analytical abilities

- Creative thinking
- Research
- Collaboration
- Communication
- Negotiation
- Accountability
- Resilience

- Metrics and data analysis
- Logical thinking
- Leadership
- Teamwork

Six Steps Model

While many people regularly solve problems using different approaches to find a solution. The most used problem-solving model is the six-step model, which addresses the many challenges that arise in the workplace. Complex challenges for teams, working groups, boards, etc., are usually solved more quickly using a shared, collaborative, and systematic approach to problem-solving.

- Step 1: Define the Problem
- Step 2: Determine the Root Cause of the Problem
- Step 3: develop alternative solutions
- Step 4: Select a solution
- Step 5: Implement the solution
- Step 6: Evaluate the outcome.

Identify the Problem. All six steps are followed as a cycle, beginning with 1. Each step must be completed before moving on to the next step.

Advantages of Sic-Step Problem Solving

The Six-Step method provides a focused problem-solving (P.S.) group procedure.

- It ensures consistency, as everyone understands the approach to be used.
- Data helps eliminate bias and preconceptions, leading to greater objectivity.
- It helps to remove divisions and encourages collaborative work.
- It stops P.S. groups from diverging into different problems.
- It also helps P.S. groups reach a consensus.
- It eliminates the confusion caused by people using different problem-solving techniques on the same issue.
- It makes the decision-making process more manageable.
- It provides a justifiable solution.

Listening

"When people talk, listen completely. Most people never listen." – Ernest Hemingway.

Listening to others is one of the most critical skills for solving problems and building a connection with someone. All leaders have experienced a situation when they are not listening, or others are not listening to them. It is called ignorance, unacceptance, and not paying respect to other people. When leaders stop listening to their people, they receive the same treatment.

Carl Rogers, a renowned American psychologist, famously stated that active and deep listening is at the core of a healthy relationship (William, 2021). Therefore, listening is so essential when it comes to solving-problem and conflicts. If you give someone your full attention and make them feel as though they're being heard and genuinely care about what they're saying, you will make them feel happy, accepted, belong, and connect with them.

In his 2003 study, Faye Doell discovered two main types of listening. We are either A, listening to understand the other person, or B, Listening to respond to the other person. Have we been conversing and knowing what to say before the other person has finished talking? I'm sure we all have at some point. This commonly happens in arguments or heated discussions where we may disagree with what someone is saying, and they say their point of view, and we'll respond with something like "Yeah, but…", and then we'll go straight into our point.

On the other hand, if we listen to understand, we are taking the opportunity to listen to what the other person is saying and how they feel. Based on what they say, we form a response that pushes the conversation further, whether we ask a question to understand what they are saying or accept it and then bring up a counterpoint.

How do we develop practical listening skills:

- **Decide to Listen**; Listening is a choice. So deciding to stop talking and start listening is an essential first step.
- **Let go of your agenda**; To truly hear someone, you must let go of your own schedule and prejudices. Focus your attention by clearing away all distractions and preconceived notions, so you can be fully present and create space in your mind for different views.
- **Be curious**; Effective listening requires you to be curious about how others see the world. Seek to understand all you can, ask open questions, and try to see the world through the other person's perception.
- **Listen with your eyes**, Maintain eye contact with the speaker, and pay attention to all the visual clues. With practice, you will become more able to read the signs and understand the meaning of what is being communicated. People will appreciate your attention and be better able to share with you.
- **Listen for the whole message;** Make sure you hear and understand the entire message before you respond. A common bad habit is listening only to what you expect to hear and then beginning rehearsing your response, ready to pitch in as soon as the dialog has stopped. (Or worse still, interrupting with an answer to what you think you are likely to hear.)
- **Be patient**; Some people take longer to find the right words, to make a point, or clarify an issue. Leave time for them to think and complete their message. Wait, and then wait some more.

- **Listen with respect;** Respecting the right to differ is a critical concept that is especially important when listening. Differences may lie in the expressed opinions or the communication style used. Remember that your non-verbal cues speak for you even when you are not communicating verbally. Listen to understand, not judge.
- **Feel empathy;** This is particularly important when people communicate something personal or painful. Empathy is more than feeling sorry for someone. Empathy requires understanding and feeling others' emotions and feelings to acknowledge the message and share your new knowledge.
- **Manage your emotions and reactions**; If what others are saying creates an emotional response in you, be attentive to listen for their words' intent and whole meaning. Don't allow others to blow wind into your sails. Remember, you have control of your reactions. Maintaining your calm, even when you feel like your 'buttons' are under pressure, is a powerful skill that will help you achieve your goals in all aspects of your life. Getting defensive and angry makes it difficult to impossible to listen.
- **Test for understanding; Periodically summarize what you** have heard of testing your understanding. Also, you will draw a more precise picture by asking questions to clarify your understanding.

Competency 9 – Innovation

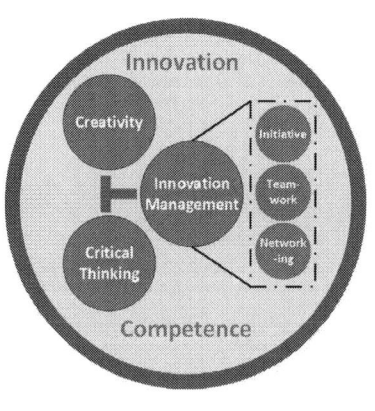

Higher Education institutions urgently need reliable, valid tools for measuring and developing an individual's capacity for innovation. Without a focus on innovation in Higher Education, graduates can leave without a valuable skill crucial to their success in the workplace. These graduates are the Future of the professions, and our future leaders - their capacity to innovate is vital.

The objective of becoming innovative is to break down into five core areas. The areas must be learned individually and linked together, causing creative thinking.

Innovation is defined as the "intentional introduction and application within a role, group or organization of ideas, processes, products or procedures." (West, 1989) It relates innovation to inventing or improving something that already exists with creativity. Students-centered learning, such as teamwork, project-based learning, active-learning, and case-study-based learning, is the best for developing innovative competencies. Therefore the development of future innovators is the primary interest of educators.

Today's concepts, such as the new economy, new technologies, and hyper-competition, explain that the dynamics of competition and markets have never been more significant. Therefore, there is a large focus on innovation in higher education learning.

Therefore, innovation should be a cross-functional learning process of activities that create innovations across higher education departments. Obviously, not only one department is responsible for innovation management activities, but all departments in the institute are responsible, so it is necessary to see how departments together create innovations.

Technology sharing is vital to the invention of all departments within the higher education institute. Technological integration refers to the integration between technologies and the product markets of the firm (Iansiti, 1997). It also emphasized the importance of satisfying the students with innovations.

Competency 10 – Organizational Awareness

Knowing your people well is vital to work through change more effectively. Reading a group's emotional currents and power relationships can improve your ability to engage and guide others in a positive direction. Also important is the ability to detect, recognize and engage in crucial social networks. These networks can be the key to getting groups to create change, build networks, and collaborate.

When inwardly focused or self-absorbed, leaders fail to read situations and organizational and external realities accurately, they will step on landmines that stall their ability to influence others, meet objectives, or even derail their careers.

Every organization has its own culture, norms, and standards of behavior. Understanding how to identify and navigate these norms is an important attribute.

- Identify the organization norms regarding attire, communication style, and etiquette.

- Adapt to organizational norms, being mindful of personal values.
- Work within the organizational hierarchy and process to address issues.

Teamwork and Collaboration, Working with others is essential to personal and professional success.

- Assume shared responsibility and accountability for collaborative work. To
- Recognize and be responsible for the needs of the group
- Delegate and negotiate within a team
- Managing a team both in face-to-face and virtual interactions
- Recruit diverse skills to a team to reach a shared goal. Recognize that various skills are needed to address complex issues.

Resource Management, Academic and professional work is frequently resource-constrained, which requires time, money, and people to manage effectively.

- Organize and effectively prioritize your work based on group constraints or resources.
- Use time management techniques to prioritize, balance, and manage workload
- Assign tasks within a group to optimize the group's work and team resources
- Develop strategies that optimize available resources to achieve an intended goal.
- Forecast work and resources required to achieve an objective

Competency 11 – Discipline

Great leaders associate discipline with a sense of peace and comfort that provide orderly conduct or pattern of behavior. Generally speaking, it is about prioritizing issues while managing the expectations of job descriptions. Leaders know the importance of discipline as they can accomplish great work by creating systems that allow them to do more faster, easier, and with less effort.

Discipline applies to leadership roles and includes staying on track with departments' and institutions' missions, visions, and values. Discipline also relates to one's character choosing the higher road, resisting those who want to pull you away from your goals, and withstanding the criticism and contempt that goes along with being in a position of power.

Many people never achieve their dreams because they fear being disciplined, and the idea of routine boars them. In routine, you will find freedom. Establishing familiar works when it becomes a habit, and you are powering through your routine on autopilot, will give you freedom because you will no longer struggle to succeed. Discipline is required in every area of life, and the lack of it can be disastrous to your life and work. Most people fail because they don't do what is required for success.

There is nothing comfortable about self-discipline unless you have a strong desire to achieve something; you will not subject yourself to the discomfort of self-discipline. It would help if you had the endurance to overcome those discomfort and mental toughness to plow through the instincts enticing you to choose the path of least resistance. You walk up just in time for work, eat when you are hungry, and sleep when you are tired.

Your life reflects your decisions, and you must make better decisions for a better future. You can have the life you desire, but it begins with taking responsibility for the state of your life at this present moment. Whether it's your finances, lifestyle, relationships, or mindset, it is up to you to make the required changes to improve. The following quote fully embodies the point I am making:

"You must take personal responsibility. You cannot change the circumstances, the seasons, or the wind, but you can change yourself." Jim Rohn

Self-discipline is a lifestyle. It's not something you use when you want to achieve a goal. Self-discipline should be embedded in your character. We look at the rich and famous and envy their lives, but it took many years of making private sacrifices to get where they are today. Your character behind closed doors is more important than what people see in public. Author, speaker, and pastor John Maxwell held a lecture at a university, and one of the students asked the following question: "John, your leadership principles sound life-changing; the problem is that I don't know anyone who will allow me to lead them. What can I do about this?" Maxwell responded, " This is an excellent question. Before you can help anyone, you must first help yourself. You can start by leading yourself."

Competency 12 – Adaptability

Adaptability is a crucial competency that refers to an individual's ability to adjust and thrive in changing circumstances, environments, and situations. It involves being open-minded, flexible, and responsive to new challenges, ideas, and approaches. Here are some key attributes and behaviors associated with adaptability:

- **Embracing Change**: Adaptable individuals are willing to embrace change and see it as an opportunity for growth and improvement rather than a hindrance. They can quickly adjust their mindset, behavior, and work processes to accommodate new circumstances.
- **Flexibility**: Adaptable individuals are flexible in their thinking and approach. They can shift gears, change strategies, and modify plans as needed without becoming overwhelmed or resistant to change. They can handle unexpected situations and adjust their priorities accordingly.
- **Learning Agility:** Adaptable individuals possess a strong desire and ability to learn and acquire new knowledge and skills. They are open to feedback, seek new information, and proactively develop their expertise to adapt to evolving demands and expectations.
- **Problem-Solving**: Adaptable individuals are resourceful and adept at problem-solving. They can analyze complex situations, identify alternative solutions, and make informed decisions even in unfamiliar or ambiguous circumstances. They remain calm and focused, finding creative ways to overcome challenges.
- **Interpersonal Adaptability:** Adaptable individuals can effectively navigate diverse interpersonal dynamics. They understand and respect different perspectives, cultures, and work styles, allowing them to collaborate effectively with individuals from various backgrounds. They can build rapport and adjust their communication and interaction style to connect with others.
- **Resilience**: Adaptable individuals demonstrate resilience in the face of adversity or setbacks. They can bounce back from failures,

learn from their experiences, and maintain a positive attitude even in challenging situations. They exhibit a strong sense of perseverance and maintain motivation despite obstacles.
- **Proactivity**: Adaptable individuals take the initiative and anticipate future changes and challenges. They stay informed about industry trends, technological advancements, and market shifts, allowing them to prepare for upcoming changes and suggest innovative solutions proactively.

Developing and demonstrating adaptability is valuable in various professional contexts, including fast-paced industries, dynamic work environments, and cross-functional teams. By continuously honing this competency, individuals can thrive in unpredictable situations and contribute to the success of their organizations.

Student successful journey

A student's journey toward success is a transformative and multifaceted process beyond mere academic achievements—including personal growth, resilience, goal setting, self-motivation, and effective utilization of resources. By addressing both academic and non-academic dimensions, students can navigate challenges, overcome obstacles, and attain holistic success during their educational journey.

Successful Transition from High School to College/University

Transitioning from high school to college or university can be a significant milestone marked by new challenges and adjustments in a student's life. This paper explores strategies to facilitate a successful transition and enable students to thrive in their new educational environment. By addressing the transition's academic, social, and personal aspects, students can navigate the complexities of college life and set a solid foundation for their academic journey.

Transitioning from high school to college/university is a pivotal period that requires students to adapt to new academic expectations, independent learning, and a diverse campus community. This section provides an overview of students' challenges during this transition and highlights the importance of implementing effective strategies for success.

Preparing for the Transition, The significance of early preparation for a smooth transition. It covers researching prospective colleges/universities, attending information sessions, and understanding admission requirements. By starting early, students can make informed decisions and align their goals with their choice of institution.

Academic Readiness, Navigating the academic landscape of college/university can be overwhelming for students. This section discusses strategies to foster academic success, including understanding academic expectations, developing time management skills, and cultivating effective study habits. It emphasizes the importance of seeking academic support through tutoring centers, writing labs, and academic advisors.

Social Integration College/university presents an opportunity to engage with a diverse community and build new relationships. This section explores strategies for social integration, such as joining student clubs, attending campus events, and connecting with classmates. It emphasizes the benefits of building relationships with professors, teaching assistants, and peers to foster a sense of belonging.

Personal Development, Transitioning to college/university involves personal growth and self-discovery. This section emphasizes strategies for personal development, including embracing diversity and new perspectives, practicing self-care, and seeking support from campus resources. It highlights the significance of maintaining a healthy work-life balance and prioritizing mental and physical well-being.

Utilizing Campus Resources, Colleges and universities offer a wide range of resources to support student success. This section explores the importance of utilizing campus resources such as libraries, research databases, technology platforms, and academic support services. It emphasizes the value of attending workshops or seminars on study skills, time management, and other relevant topics.

Transitioning from High School Culture, High school culture differs from college/university culture, requiring students to adapt to new norms and expectations. This section discusses strategies for transitioning from the high school culture to the college/university culture, including embracing independence, taking ownership of one's learning, and practicing effective communication and advocacy skills.

Case Studies and Success Stories provide practical insights success stories of students who have successfully navigated the transition from high school to college/university. These examples highlight the strategies they implemented and the outcomes they achieved.

The transition from high school to college/university is a transformative journey that requires careful planning and the implementation of effective strategies. By adopting strategies that address academic readiness, social integration, personal development, and campus resource utilization, students can set a solid foundation for success in their college/university experience. Students can thrive and achieve their academic goals with determination, support, and implementation of these strategies.

Student's Mindset for Academic Success: Cultivating a Growth Mindset

The mindset with which students approach their academic pursuits plays a crucial role in their overall success. This paper explores the concept of a growth mindset and its impact on academic achievement. It delves into strategies for cultivating a growth mindset, overcoming self-limiting beliefs, embracing challenges, seeking growth opportunities, and fostering resilience. Students can unlock their full potential and achieve academic success by adopting a growth mindset.

The importance of mindset in academic success introduces the concept of a growth mindset, highlighting its essential characteristics and impact on student motivation, learning, and achievement. The section emphasizes the role of mindset in shaping students' beliefs about their abilities and potential for growth.

The student's Self-limiting beliefs can hinder academic success; It emphasizes the importance of self-reflection, challenging negative thoughts, and reframing failures as learning experiences. Students are encouraged to replace self-doubt with self-belief and embrace a positive, growth-oriented perspective.

Accepting challenges: A growth mindset encourages students to accept rather than avoid them. Challenge themselves academically by developing problem-solving skills, increasing resilience, and expanding knowledge. Strategies for overcoming challenges are identified, such as setting ambitious goals, seeking intellectual stimulation, and persevering in the face of difficulty.

Effort and persistence are key elements of a growth mindset. This section emphasizes prioritizing effort over innate talent and understanding that sustained practice leads to improvement. Strategies for maintaining a solid work ethic, effective time management, and sustaining motivation are discussed.

A growth mindset encourages students to actively seek opportunities for growth and learning. This section discusses the importance of seeking feedback, accepting constructive criticism, and continuously improving. Strategies for seeking challenging courses, participating in extracurricular activities, and pursuing personal interests are identified.

Resilience is essential for overcoming school challenges. This section focuses on strategies for building resilience, such as developing problem-solving skills, cultivating a positive attitude, seeking peer and mentor support, and self-care. Students are encouraged to view setbacks as temporary obstacles and to emerge stronger from academic setbacks.

A growth mindset thrives in a supportive learning environment. This section emphasizes the role of teachers, parents, and peers in fostering a growth mindset. Strategies for creating a supportive environment are discussed, such as providing constructive feedback, encouraging collaboration, and recognizing effort and progress.

Metacognitive skills, such as self-reflection, goal setting, and self-regulation, are essential for academic success. This section focuses on strategies for developing metacognitive skills, such as setting clear learning goals, monitoring progress, and reflecting on learning strategies. Students are encouraged to take an active role in their learning process.

Cultivating a growth mindset is a powerful tool for achieving academic success. Students can unlock their full potential by embracing challenges, valuing effort and persistence, seeking growth opportunities, and developing resilience. Educators, parents, and peers play a crucial role in creating.

Student Success

Student success is a multifaceted concept that goes beyond academic performance. It encompasses various factors, including engagement, well-being, personal development, and the acquisition of essential skills. This topic explores strategies and approaches to foster student success and support students in achieving their academic goals while nurturing their holistic growth.

1. Creating a Supportive Learning Environment:
   - Build a positive, inclusive school culture that promotes respect, diversity, and belonging.
   - Establish supportive relationships between students, teachers, and staff members.
   - Provide resources and services that address students' academic, social, emotional, and physical needs.
   - Promote a safe, nurturing environment that encourages risk-taking, exploration, and self-expression.

2. Academic Support and Skill Development:
   - Implement effective instructional practices that cater to diverse learning styles and abilities.
   - Offer targeted interventions and enrichment programs to address individual students' academic needs.

- Provide opportunities for students to develop essential skills such as critical thinking, problem-solving, communication, and collaboration.
- Encourage self-directed learning and foster a growth mindset among students.

3. Student Engagement and Involvement:

- Promote active student participation in learning activities through interactive teaching methods, group projects, and hands-on experiences.
- Encourage student involvement in extracurricular activities, clubs, sports, and community service.
- Provide opportunities for student leadership and empower students to have a voice in decision-making processes.
- Cultivate a love for learning and curiosity through stimulating and relevant educational experiences.

4. Effective Support Systems:

- Implement comprehensive academic advising and career counseling services to guide students' educational and career pathways.
- Offer mentoring programs that pair students with supportive adults or peer mentors who provide guidance, encouragement, and advice.
- Establish partnerships with families, community organizations, and local businesses to enhance student support networks and broaden opportunities for students.

5. Assessment and Feedback:

- Implement formative and summative assessments that provide timely and constructive feedback to guide student learning.
- Use data-driven approaches to identify areas of improvement and implement targeted interventions.
- Encourage self-reflection and goal-setting among students to monitor their progress and promote continuous growth.

Enhancing student success requires a comprehensive approach focusing on academic achievement, personal growth, and overall well-being. By creating a supportive learning environment, providing academic support, fostering student engagement, establishing effective support systems, and implementing meaningful assessment practices, educational institutions can empower students to thrive academically and holistically. Investing in student success contributes to individual achievement, strengthens the overall educational experience, and prepares students for future success in their academic and professional endeavors.

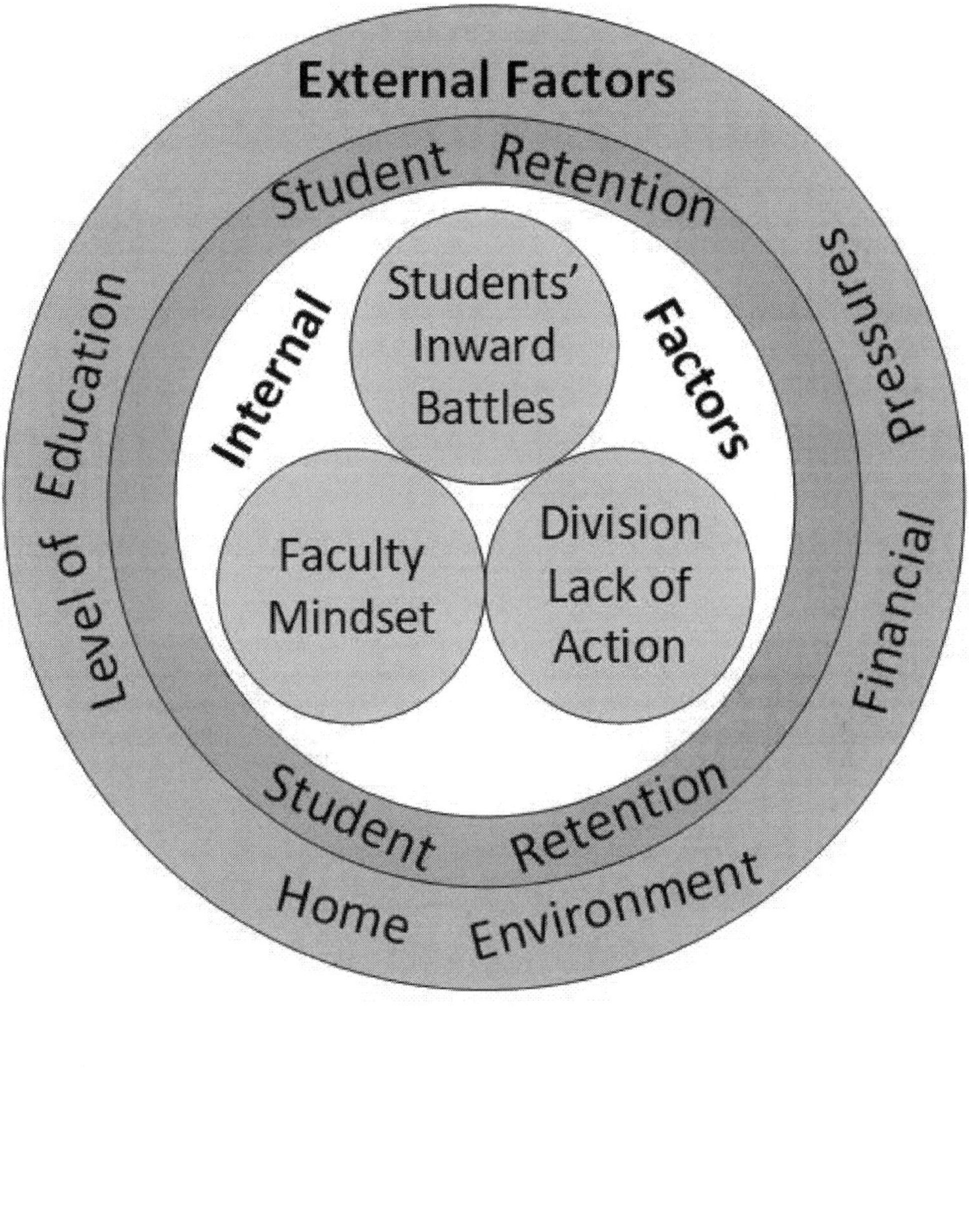
External Factors
Student Retention
Level of Education
Financial pressures
Internal Factors
Students' Inward Battles
Faculty Mindset
Division Lack of Action
Student Retention
Home Environment

Retention

The most prominent challenge community colleges face today is serving traditionally underrepresented populations and students who would not otherwise have the opportunity to attend college. These students need assistance developmentally, academically, and socially. Meanwhile, assisting the performance gap among underrepresented populations.

Another retention issue is facing Community colleges with students who are the first in their families to attempt a college education. They often do not have the study skills, discipline, cultural capital, or previous educational experiences to position them for success.

The importance of student integration (both socially and academically) is that sense of belonging to a group of people keeps them motivated and attached to their academic work leading to a higher probability of commitment and retention. Retention rates are related to the interaction between the students attending the college and the characteristics of the college.

Students' beliefs are affected by the interaction between the students and the community college's different activities and stimulus components.

Too often, we blame the victim and avoid seeing our actions as at least partially responsible for the problems we face. It is easy to see the absence of student success as solely the responsibility of students or external forces beyond institutional control. I see three influential internal factors at work: student retention, students' inward battles, faculty mindset, and Division lack of Action. And three significant external factors are home environment, financial reason, and Level of Education.

Every student has Internal and external factors that lead to a retention decrease. The division's responsibility is to help in students' stability, which leads to educational commitment toward graduation.

Internal Factors

Our world has changed in many ways, birthing pressures that yielded confusion and uncertainty. Family life has shifted from the collective to individualism. Life has changed as we know it, and our students are confused amidst debates over diversity, equity, inclusion, multiculturalism, and political correctness in life and academics.

As an educator who witnessed ignorance and favoritism amidst self-deceptive academics, and students, I understand their battles. We live in a multicultural society, refusing to understand and accept each other, so we call upon tolerance as a solution, where every person is an island with self-governing guidelines.

We all ignore one basic fact: "Life is Change." It is about students who want to change, students who do not know how to change, students who need help to change, students who resist change, and students who seem unable to leave their current circumstances and accept the support of others to change.

Students need transformational instruction with practical assignments, leading to habitual action and lasting success. We must teach our students to set realistic expectations and goals to produce a conventional system to sustain those goals, focus on success rather than failures, expect relapses, be aware of tempting situations, and get support from trusted entities.

Change is difficult; therefore, students resist change even though they want it and need it. They are unwilling to give up what is safe, predictable, and familiar; They have no absolute conviction that change is healthier than the status quo; they fear what lies ahead and convince themselves that it is not realistic or practical.

Experience in community colleges has taught us that students are unique in personality, culture, and how they perceive others. As an educator and lifelong student, I observed students' diversity as they walked through my classroom and campus. When students arrive at the community college gates, life has somehow damaged them. These damages come from family/cultural life, school lack of Action, inappropriate instruction, and the danger of community pressures.

One of two things will happen, community college adds to the student's burden to the point that the student leaves and lose their way, or they find encouragement, positive challenge, and a community of friendships and hope of success breaking away the shackles of the past.

Students' Inward Battles

Students who have enrolled in higher education are bound to encounter specific issues that they are not comfortable with and cannot deal with efficiently. As all students are different, they will have various issues affecting their education and academic goals.

Data analyses indicated eight main learning challenges faced by students in higher education: cognitive challenge, becoming an active learner, coping with reading materials, instructional problems, language barrier, time management, the burden of assignments, and cultural difference in higher education. Besides this, most students, if not all, suffer from one thing or another; some are superficial, and others are profoundly concerned.

Generally, most students avoid inward battles like the plague. They see it, as usual, as negative energy or emotional attacks. Consequently, many students suffering from inward struggles either suppress, deny, or withdraw from circumstances that exaggerate the situation or believe it does not exist. The truth is that the desire to satisfy the needs of their temperament is the cause of these battles.

If students in life face confusion, uncertainty, frustration, and abuse in their phases of human development, stresses and disruption are imminent. More likely, students were misunderstood, ignored, used, and marked as worthless and insignificant, and damage will occur.

Students walk into our classes with bags of past and current damages. We can not solve most of the student's battles; however, acceptance and respect open the door to dialogue. Classroom observation provides the following adverse facts about damaged students:

- Inability to make up their minds at any particular moment
- Value the opinion of others than their own
- Does not accept their point of view as valid and significant
- Always doubts their credibility
- Has no stable mindset
- Does not feel challenged and is quickly bound into guilt
- Cannot make a decision and stick by it, and always seek the support of others to bolster their point

- Is uncertain about their thought process and how to go about achieving their purpose
- Social anxiety and separation
- Self-centered and unreceptive
- Prominent(Depression, Anxiety, Anger, Guilt, Forgiveness, Loneliness), development, Interpersonal(Conflict and relationship, Abuse and Neglect), Identity(Inferiority and Self-Esteem, Physical Illness, and Grief), Family, Control(Mental Disorder, Addiction, Financial, and Vocational), and Future Issues.

Issues students face on campus.
- New-Admits or Transferred Students think about how they will handle the school environment with other students and teachers. They are more concerned with such issues than studying, which hampers their performance.
- One of life's most challenging things is coping with illness and pain. In some ways, it can be even more complex when a student has to look after an ill loved one than with their disease.
- Sex is powerful and dangerous if it does not run in the correct channels and safety procedures are not used. Many of the problems about sex come because of ignorance. Students do not understand the purpose of sex and how it should be used. The effects of internet pornography, magazines, films, T.V., books, and advertisements have created a wrong picture of sex. Young people are pressured to have sex experience before they are ready.
- Another major problem faced by many students is Bullying. Seniors and other students often have the habit of dominating a

newcomer or someone they do not like. Such behavior leaves mental scars on the mind of the students.
- Suicide is a very grave problem that needs special attention. Low percentages, failure, harsh punishment, and Bullying are the leading causes.
- Weakness in specific disciplines is a common problem faced by the majority. Genuine hatred for certain subjects like Maths and Ineffective teaching methods of certain teachers are the leading causes.

Faculty and Institution Mindset

Before Covid19, colleges often relied on students to request accommodations instead of taking the institutional initiative to identify and remove barriers to their success. The decrease in enrollment and retention has forced many issues the student has been suffering from silently to the surface as one of the major issues causing these barriers to retention and student success.

Institutional services are the key to students' success. In reality, many institutions are forcing these services on faculty and staff rather than providing the needed services by increasing their resources to ensure student success. Sadly, these institutions suffer from self-deception, reaping what they have Sowed.

Neurodivergent students are traumatized upon arrival to community college as needed services are dysfunctional. Institutions enroll staff who are qualified on paper but disqualified in function. The institute is responsible for developing its staff to alleviate their skill and provide the proper services.

Faculty can help these students by not treating them differently but by providing solutions. Breaking significant assignments into smaller parts reduces their stress and makes tasks reachable. Faculty who reuse topic assignments without assessing the students can be damaging.

Grades assessment allocation is vital to students' success. Speaking from experience, in the early 90s, the writer suffered from memory issues due to a head injury. Work rating was not measured correctly, 10% assignments and 90% final exam. I suffered for two years without consideration, even though the accommodation was requested but not given, because faculty were too busy with their research.

Reading and writing are an American dysfunction. I am heartbroken to see our students unable to read and write their language, never mind learning a foreign one. The persisting environment is a deciding factor in their thriving or declining. We have no right to brand our students unless we have solutions to their predicament. Reading and writing have long been problematic in higher education; while HE offered focused developmental classes in the past now has been abandoned due to cutbacks.

Reading and writing issues did not rise in higher education; the situation started from grade one to twelve. Discussing these issues with school teachers, I get the same answer. School administration expects the teachers to be educators, child counselors, and disability service professionals, and all services combined by refusing to provide the necessary resources to the students. In addition, the administration continues to demand passing grades from the teachers reflecting false reality.

Community College needs more resource allocation by hiring more service providers to aid students along the way to success. Each student must have a success plan from day one involving all the service departments in the college working together to ensure successful progression.

The industry's demand for strong written communication skills is soaring, and as a result, our graduates face blockading reality when they apply for work. The challenge has accelerated as community colleges gain a diverse population of students, including a growing percentage of nontraditional students.

"The demand placed on writing is only increasing, yet the support institutions are giving students to communicate effectively is not," said Dorian Stone, the head of organizations revenue at Grammarly, an AI-powered communication assistant trusted by over 3,000 institutions. "As a result, a larger gap exists today than ever before for the quality of written communication and the value placed upon it in a student's higher ed experience."

Most virtual interactions occur in written form — through papers that replace presentations, discussions in chat forums, reactions to other students' blog posts, and email communications with instructors. According to HIGHER ED DIVE, This shift to remote education due to COVID-19 has made written communication and reading skills critical to student success. If institutions aren't trying to help develop writing skills and increase support, their students are disadvantaged.

In a recent study by Grammarly, 92% of participating college educators said students struggled with confidence in their writing. There were several areas of concern: 80% of participants believed students lacked the skills to appropriately communicate in writing with university faculty and staff, and 79% said they struggled with peer communication. These alarming figures come as writing needs are increasing, with many instructors making online courses more interactive.

Even though the problem originated before college enrollment, we must find solutions to help our students succeed. The question is, what are the steps we need to take?

- Pre-starting semester course
- Use ESL teaching skills to help American-speaking students improve their reading and writing.
- Community Colleges should provide Grammarly software to help their students with writing skills. Grammarly helps students find and correct low-level errors in their written work and avoid unintentional plagiarism. Requiring students to check their results in Grammarly before turning them in allows instructors to focus more on higher-level issues such as critical thinking, creativity, and demonstration of learning.
- Provide digital books for students to use and listen to as they read.
- Provide reading and writing skills to parents
- Provide tutorials to help students with their work

Faculty

- Identify and explain the skills used in active reading.
- Provide a short video/voice message explaining all assignments
- Summarization of what students have heard or read. Short sentences.
- Write questions to answers
- Identifying the main idea and theme

Faculty, staff, and administration operate from two distinct mindsets: self-focused inward and outward-focused. If our focus is student success, we must shift our perspectives, equipping our employees to invite outward mindset ways; and helping leaders turn organizational systems and processes outward to encourage and reward sustained systemic change.

Goals are good for setting a direction, but systems and habits are best for making progress and maintaining success.

1. **Winners and Losers have the same goals.**

    If successful and unsuccessful people share the same goals, then the goal can not be what differentiates the winners from the losers.

2. **Achieving a goal is only a momentary change.**

    Imagine you have a messy room and set a goal to clean it. You will have a clean room if you summon the energy to tidy up. But if you maintain the same messy habits that led to a messy room in the first place, soon you'll be looking at a new pile of clutter and hoping for another burst of motivation. You're left chasing the same outcome because you never changed the system behind it. You treated a symptom without addressing the root cause.

    Achieving a goal changes your life momentarily. Goals or results are not the cause of the problem. We need to solve the root problems at the system level to improve and maintain desired results. Fix the input, and the output will fix itself.

    How many of us set a goal to lose weight, and shortly after we successfully reach our goal, we regain the weight again? Why? Thou we have reached our destination, our eating habits have not changed, so we regain the weight. We must follow the system to achieve the goal and keep working on it as a new way of life. Thus a new habit is formed, and success will become the norm.

The same with retention; we work hard to gain success, but we fall back into our old habits, and our retention number decrees again.

Solutions and strategies

Extensive research indicates that neither holding students back a grade nor promoting them unprepared fosters achievement. Studies suggest retention negatively impacts students' behavior, attitude, and attendance. Social promotion undermines students' futures when they fail to develop critical studies and job-related skills (Denton, 2001; U.S. Department of Education, 1999). In contrast, recent research and practice indicate that alternative strategies, which strike at the root causes of poor performance, offer genuine hope for helping all students succeed. These strategies are: intensify learning, provide professional development to assure skilled teachers, expand learning options, assess students to assist teachers, and intervene to arrest poor performance.

An issue of concern in higher education institutions worldwide is students' retention and success in their studies. This is a particularly pressing issue regarding widening participation for under-represented student groups, increasing student diversity, and educational quality assurance and accountability processes.

Strategies

- Support with collective college services and guide students from admission to graduation, starting with the "Understanding Your Success Experience course."
- Be innovative and address the diverse support needs of students
- Leverage digital options to build communities and engagement
- Identify at-risk students early
- Leverage technology to improve the student experience
- Intensify learning through rigorous standards, rich curriculum, effective teachers, and meaningful learning.
- Provide Professional Development to ensure skilled teachers.
- Expand learning options
- Assess informing faculty
- Intervene early and often

Promoting Student engagements

Promoting student engagement is essential for creating a dynamic and effective learning environment. Here are some strategies to promote student engagement:

- **Active learning:** Encourage active participation by incorporating group discussions, hands-on projects, problem-solving exercises, and debates. These activities allow students to apply their knowledge, think critically, and engage with the subject.

- **Technology integration**: Utilize technology tools and resources to enhance student engagement. This can include interactive presentations, educational apps, online discussion boards, virtual field trips, and multimedia content. Technology provides opportunities for students to explore concepts in innovative and engaging ways.

- **Real-world connections**: Connect the curriculum to real-life situations and current events. Show students how their learning content is relevant and applicable to their world. This helps students see the value and purpose of their education, leading to increased engagement.

- **Varied instructional methods:** Incorporate various strategies to cater to different learning styles and preferences. Some students may excel with visual aids, while others prefer hands-on activities or auditory instruction. You can engage a broader range of students by using diverse teaching methods.

- **Student choice and autonomy**: Provide opportunities for students to make choices within their learning. They can select project topics, provide assignment options, or incorporate student-led discussions. When students have a sense of ownership and autonomy, they are more likely Students with a sense of ownership and autonomy engaged and invested in their learning.

- **Formative assessment and feedback**: Regularly assess students' understanding through formative assessments, such as quizzes, discussions, or short assignments. Provide timely and constructive feedback to help students track their progress and make necessary improvements. This feedback loop encourages active participation and engagement in the learning process.

- **Collaborative learning**: Foster a collaborative learning environment where students work together on projects, group assignments, or problem-solving tasks. Collaboration promotes engagement through peer interaction, shared responsibility, and the exchange of ideas. It also helps develop essential teamwork and communication skills.

- **Encourage questions and curiosity**: Create a safe and supportive classroom environment that encourages students to ask questions, share their thoughts, and pursue their curiosity. Foster a culture of inquiry by valuing and rewarding curiosity. This helps students become active learners, driving their engagement with the subject matter.

- **Gamification**: Incorporate gamification elements into the learning process to make it more interactive and enjoyable. This can include using educational games, leaderboards, badges, or rewards to motivate and engage students. Gamification can make the learning experience more immersive and foster healthy student competition.

- **Personalized learning**: Recognize and accommodate students' interests, strengths, and learning needs. Provide opportunities for personalized learning experiences, such as independent projects or differentiated assignments. When students feel their unique needs are considered, they are more likely to engage and take ownership of their learning.

Goals

- Provide the teaching staff chance to participate in professional development opportunities.
- Challenging coursework is offered to develop high-achieving students.
- Assessments identify areas where learning problems exist.

- Supported learning by expanded learning programs, such as lower class size at the primary level, structures that group children and teachers for extended periods, and year-round schools.
- Students have multiple learning opportunities through extended learning time, differentiated instruction, early intervention, and ongoing assessment.
- Early intervention programs stop the cycle of failure and accelerate learning.

Action plans

Administrators can take the following steps to produce higher achievement:

- Create professional development plans to ensure that teachers receive best practices training.
- Provide time for teachers to work together and coach each other in applying effective instructional techniques.
- Hire reading specialists to address the needs of struggling readers — especially in the freshman stage.
- Hire highly trained teachers to provide intervention for at-risk populations.
- Provide high-quality summer programs with follow-up intervention during the school year.

Teachers can do the following to bring about successful learning environments:

- Use creative and flexible scheduling to extend learning time for students who need it.
- Create classrooms that accommodate different learning styles.

- Use ongoing, performance-based assessment to guide daily teaching decisions.
- Create intervention programs that accelerate learning and extend learning time for students.

Success Experience Course

The Success Experience Course should be designed for today's students who are increasingly jb-focused, skilled in using technology, and concerned about the future.

Help students get the most out of their time in college. Success Experience Course addresses the needs of the broadest possible range of students through its content coverage and organization, activities, assessment, and design. Using a research-driven approach informed by decades of information on the first-year experience, the author team provides students who need the most support with the practical help necessary to flourish in college, life, and their chosen careers. Students matter, and the college should devote its professional focus to them.

Course Goal
This class aims to transform students' academic behaviors and create a learning environment to integrate students into a collegiate environment, ensure college readiness, enhance overall performance in college courses, and facilitate the successful completion of a degree or certificate.

Course Overview
This course serves as the College first-year experience student success course. It is designed to provide first-year students with an opportunity to attain complete college and life success. It will assist students in

realizing their full potential by facilitating activities that promote effective learning and personal and professional growth. This course aims to achieve this goal by helping new students connect with college resources and promote a positive and successful college experience that leads to completion.

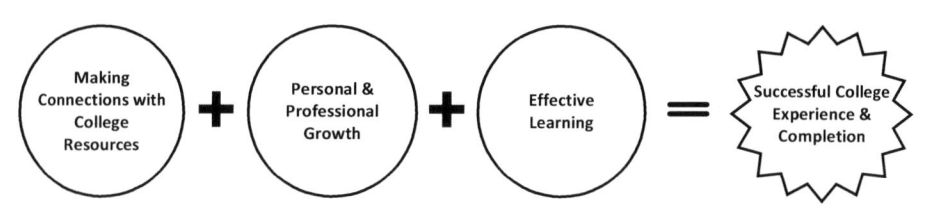

Making Connections with College Resources + Personal & Professional Growth + Effective Learning = Successful College Experience & Completion

A study of the research and theory in the psychology of learning, cognition, and motivation; factors that impact learning; and application of learning strategies. Theoretical models of strategic learning, cognition, and motivation serve as the conceptual basis for introducing college-level student academic strategies. Students developing these skills should be able to continually draw from the theoretical models they have learned. Students use assessment instruments (e.g., learning inventories) to help them identify their strengths and weaknesses as strategic learners. Students are ultimately expected to integrate and apply the learning skills discussed across their academic programs and become effective and efficient learners.

Student Learning Outcomes
1. Students in the college success course will be able to identify, describe, and utilize campus support services, systems, and student life opportunities.
2. Students in the college success course will be able to use financial literacy knowledge and skills to create a personal money management plan for college success.

3. Students in the college success course will be able to establish collegial relationships with College faculty, staff, and peers.
4. Students in the college success course will be able to assess and report on their strengths, preferences, and college and career success attributes.
5. Students in the college success course will be able to formulate educational and career goals and apply strategies to advance their goals and college performance.
6. Students in the college success course will be able to create an academic plan and identify the requirements for completing their educational program.

Course Objectives

Students will:

1. Identify, discuss, and evaluate learning and study strategies as they apply to the academic environment.
2. Examine personal goals and career plans, utilize college resources, including all components of the student portal and learning management system (D2L), and apply strategies for academic success.
3. Identify types of financial aid and criteria to receive and maintain funding.
4. Exhibit written and verbal communication skills individually and in groups.
5. Assess ideas, principles, and patterns related to personal life situations.
6. Design a strategy for success.

The student's statement of purpose
is concise, clear, and well-written, demonstrating their specific academic or professional goal—a reminder of WHY they are in higher education, their outcome, and the consequences of not achieving that outcome. (Make it visible), where the student can see it every day for motivation.

- The reason for college?
- Why did you choose this specific program?
- What profession are you seeking?
- What are your milestones?

Scheduled academic adviser's meetings
- Manage and inform studies progress, and discuss problems and needs. Meet once a month.
- Maintain open communication, establish and build relationships, and establish personalized support services.
- Discuss future events and prepare for it
- Use the following grid for record keeping.

Topic	What I know	What I want to know	What I learned
(Example)			
Milestone?	I need it for goal completion.	How to create a milestone?	Step-by-step instructions for creating milestones.

Create Good Habits

As we form our habits, we will discover that keeping bad habits is more manageable than building good ones. Students' inward battles and pressures keep devouring their development. Bad habits they have acquired through the years will only fade away in the practice of good habits. Students' actions contribute to their behavior and the character they wish to become. Each small habit that they develop motivates change in their lives.

According to James Clear, there are four steps to habit formation:

1. **The cue** triggers our brain to start a behavior. The student's mind continually looks for internal and external sources of rewards; the cue predicts a reward.
2. **Cravings** motivate a habit. Students do not crave the habit itself but desire the change the students experience when they form a habit.
3. **Response**, This step refers to the habit students perform. It depends on their level of motivation, the amount of effort they are willing to apply, and their ability to execute the action.
4. **Reward**, A reward has a two-pronged purpose. The first is to satisfy your craving, and the second is to teach us which actions are helpful and worth remembering.

Consideration

1. A habit is a behavior repeated often to become automatic.
2. Habits aim to solve life problems with as little energy as possible.
3. The habit loop has four steps: cue, cravings, response, and reward.
4. There are Four Laws of Behavior Change you can apply in improving habits: (a) Make it obvious, (b) Make it attractive, (c) Make it easy, and (d) Make it satisfying.

The four rules are as follows; the first two (Cue and Craving) are the problem phase, and the second (Response and Reward) is the solving phase.

Rule	To Form a Good Habit	To Break a Bad Habit	Relevant
1st	Make it obvious	Make it invisible	Cue
2nd	Make it attractive	Make it unattractive	Cravings
3rd	Make it easy	Make it difficult	Response
4th	Make it satisfying	Make it unsatisfying	Reward

Strategies to increase the effectiveness in enrollment, retention, and completion of Information Technology academic programs

Community colleges facing enrollment recovery, retention, and completion must take bold and steadfast actions to lead through dynamic change for competitive action.

Deliver education, training, and certification credentials to develop the most competitive workforce.

Strategy 1: Regular engagement with workforce leaders to leverage industry hard-to-fill jobs.

Strategy 2: Develop a dynamic curriculum with business state demands to get students jobs.

Strategy 3: Establish faculty professional development to advance their competencies and information technology pedagogies.

Strategy 4: Develop and transform programs and faculty improvement to meet the workforce's on-demand needs.

> **Tactic 1:** IT faculty professional development events
>
> **Tactic 2:** Implement innovative technology (Specific, Measurable, Attainable, Results-oriented, and Time-bound)
>
> **Tactic 3:** Use challenge-driven innovation methodology, Discover (Gather problems and insights). Define (Areas to focus on), Develop (Potential solutions), and Deliver solutions

Increase enrollment of students in career and technical courses and programs through customized corporate training

Strategy 1: Expand the physical footprint of the Information Technology department to new locations to deliver appropriate course offerings to meet emerging programmatic needs and elevate services.

Strategy 2: Enhance the department's presence in the community by increasing awareness, cultivating relationships, building partnerships, and developing offerings resources to respond to current and future needs

Strategy 3: Provide resources to our community to enroll and complete a career-based program of study

> **Tactic 1**: Provide credit and non-course offerings at the employer's premises as needed
>
> **Tactic 2**: Provide Bootcamp certification programs at regular intervals, enhancing knowledge tangibility
>
> **Tactic 3**: attract new populations of students into IT career and technical programs
>
> **Tactic 4**: Ensure Information Technology Academy facilities are well-maintained

Ensure a high level of IT enrollment, retention, and completion

Strategy 1: Peer interactions and association to influence student's cognitive development, self-confidence, and motivation

Strategy 2: Boost marketing to prospective students

Strategy 2: Expand participation of students in career planning

Strategy 3: Cultivate a sense of commitment and determination to achieve the learning

Strategy 4: New student orientation programs that promote diversity are the gateway to student's inclusiveness in academia

Strategy 5: Introduce the Student Mentoring system, utilizing the best second-year students to mentor first-year students.

> **Tactic 1**: Create and develop workshops, tutoring, and mentoring system to improve student learning and study skills
>
> **Tactic 2:** Focus on opportunities the career opportunity
>
> **Tactic 3**: Create a safe working environment where students and faculty can interact in a professional relationship aiming at students' success
>
> **Tactic 4**. Provide academic and social support outside the classroom, supporting inclusion and cultural differences
>
> **Tactic 5**: Frequent evaluation of progress and offering further guidance to students
>
> **Tactic 6**: Reach out to the enrollment of underrepresented and non-traditional students

Alignment of credit and noncredit courses as a stepping stone to additional education and training that leads to higher earnings and greater career sustainability

Strategy 1: Award credit for prior learning

Strategy 2: Introduce adult learners to career change

> **Tactic 1:** Recognize credentials from passed certification exams
>
> **Tactic 2**: Recognize and align continuing education noncredit courses as credited through outcome comparison.
>
> **Tactic 3**: Award credit through the prior learning experience

Tactic 4: Military Education

Tactic 5: Apprenticeship

Tactic 6: Develop an accelerated program to decrease degree/course completion

Tactic 7: Prepare to offer alternative assessments, intervention processes, and assistance

ENROLLMENT—Creating Opportunities

Today's higher education recruitment landscape—shaped by the pandemic—has enrollment leaders using every trick in their playbook to meet their student enrollment goals. So how can enrollment managers figure out which college enrollment strategies will work and which will eat up time and energy with little to show for it?

Community colleges seeking solutions facing enrollment challenges must be willing to take drastic measures to reach their desired outcome. In an era where student demographics, behaviors, and even level of participation, it's more complicated than ever before to find, engage, and enroll our best-fit students.

Community colleges must drive progress on institutional priorities with resources, implementation support, and expert advice. Navigate's workflow solutions help academic advisors, faculty, and staff scale interventions, streamline day-to-day work, and create a truly coordinated network for student success.

Empower students to take charge of their success. Creating a navigating mobile app provides the structure for the college journey and proactive guidance at students' pivotal moments. Navigate's student interface helps you connect with students on their terms, building a profound sense of purpose at the Community College.

To achieve student success, we must eliminate persistent equity gaps at our community colleges. Our communities will thrive if everyone has a fair and equal chance to gain the knowledge and skills necessary to succeed.

Early Recruitment Activities

Begin our student recruitment activities as early as possible. Contacting students early on often generates more enrollments. Students who are contacted as sophomores are more likely to enroll than students who are approached as seniors. Get actionable insights to include students' level of interest in the community college.

College-bound students use an expanding range of channels to research and engage with schools they're considering. The corresponding challenge for enrollment leaders is understanding where and how to connect with them.

Create a recruitment-marketing portfolio for each interested prospective student, advancing the enrollment goals with minimal redundancy. The aim of the enrolment recruitment pinpoint three areas: 1. Finding students to recruit; 2. Getting actionable insights on them; 3. And moving them through the funnel.

Personalize student communications

To eventually get students to enroll at the campus, we must enrich their interests throughout their college search journey. Such an approach will engage students *and their families* over time by ensuring they receive the correct information, in the proper format, at the right moment.

Involve Parents and guardians in the college search.

Parents play an essential role in a student's college enrollment journey. According to EAB data research, parents have become the top influencers since the pandemic. Students and parents work together in their search for the right college. Therefore, the college needs to communicate with the parents helping them find information, fill gaps, and build a relationship with them during the early stages of their research.

Parents are looking for:

- Safety for their college children, including physical, intellectual, and mental
- Academic Reputation and knowing
    - what college graduates are doing gives an idea of their children's future
    - And how they are involved in the community.
    - What are their alumni talking about the college?
- They care about the college website, which is the first line of attraction. How easy it is to find information about the school, its academic and activities
- Allowing the parents to walk around the campus and see for themselves at any moment. Physical visits are more important than virtual visits in narrowing down their choices.

Make the students, not our college, the focal point of our recruitment messaging

many colleges prioritize talking to prospective students about their school—what it has to offer, what the campus culture is like, and what makes it unique and special. But this is one of the most common mistakes I see colleges make.

From the start, we must express our belief that students come first. We show the students that they matter and that we are the bridge to help them reach their goals. Listen to their dreams, let them express them, and then show them how we can make them come true.

Integrating media strategy

Web, outdoor, search, streaming audio, connected Television—today's prospective students move effortlessly across media channels and devices, anticipating you to show up consistently in all of them. This new reality requires a plan that treats media—in all its forms—as an integrated, cohesive system with the student journey at the very center.

Media is a powerful tool for building a brand and a funnel, but doing it right requires experience, skill, and unbending attention to detail. We need to identify new opportunities and evaluate them.

We need to leverage buying power, place the right message in front of the right prospects, and continually measure and optimize ad placement.

Digital Advertising

New digital advertising technologies are dynamic in nature. Colleges must unlock the latest digital advertising platforms and reach prospective students at crucial points in their decision-making process.

- **Paid Search:** Use paid placement to appear on search engine results on pages when prospects look at colleges online.
- **Retargeting:** Stay at the top of our website visitors' minds after they leave by using targeted, tailored ads.
- **Display:** Use geotargeting and segmentation to target audiences while they browse other websites.
- **Streaming Video:** Elevate our brand and make a compelling impression on our audience with placed video ads.
- **Streaming Radio:** Heighten our awareness among our prospects with placement on platforms like Spotify and Pandora.
- **Paid Social Media:** Target and engage with our optimal next-class members on the platforms they frequent.

Search Engine Optimization (SEO)

Good SEO is part science, part art, and 100 percent strategy. Done right, it can help us reach and attract our best-fit students. Search engine rules and algorithms change constantly, so effective SEO requires staying on top of the latest information and acting accordingly. Whether tweaking our website's copy and code or optimizing our profiles on third-party sites, attentive SEO maintenance is an important marketing tool.

- **SEO Content:** Ensure content that satisfies search engines and prospective students.

- **Link Building:** Build a digital reputation with links to the site from other articles and online listings.
- **Technical SEO:** Keep the website's codebase, speed, and status codes updated with search engines' preferences.

Measurement, Reporting, and Optimization

Effective optimization depends on effective measurement and reporting. Bring data together for better and more data-driven decision-making.

Dual enrollment

Since the beginning of the epidemic, colleges have been challenged to focus on anything beyond their immediate consequences. It is time to pause and take a collection of complete reshaping facing community colleges. Such trends will have long-term impacts on how community colleges interact with students, and getting ahead of them will position them for success in the future.

Increased competitions

Community college enrollment faces several new external threats outside of the traditional competition from other colleges. Our prospective and current students are likely evaluating the perceived value of our community college against other factors.

As students cast a wider net when considering their options, community colleges must make early, meaningful interactions with students, follow up with inquiries, and create a recruitment communications strategy that will allow them to stand out against the other options the student might be considering.

Capitalizing on dual enrollment rebounds

Many community colleges felt some relief in the fall of 2022 as enrollment declines began to alleviate and improve. This enrollment recovery was welcomed after losing students during the pandemic due to reductions in new students and a national dip in retention.

Knowing that dual enrollment is crucial to continuing stabilization efforts, community colleges must double down on substantial high school partnerships and measures that help retain dual-enrolled students into programs leading to a degree. This is especially important as younger students are reconsidering their pathways after high school, which increasingly may lead them into the workforce or an alternative credential.

Increased unmet basic needs & mental health concerns

According to a recent 2022 CCSSE report (CCCSE, 2022), community college students' mental health worsens, and many students struggle with basic needs like housing and food. Unfortunately, the number of community college students considering stopping college because of mental stress has more than doubled from 24% in 2020 to 63% in 2021.

Contributors to these mental health concerns might be tied partly to basic needs stressors. For example, 27% of community college students reported having difficulty paying their rent or mortgage in the past year, and 21% have skipped or reduced meals. It's easy to understand how these barriers make it impossible for students to start, or finish, their education without deliberate support from student affairs professionals. Therefore, community colleges need to invest in basic needs to stabilize enrollment.

Pell Grant availability for incarcerated adults

Starting in July 2023, over 700,000 incarcerated adults (Mangan, 2022) will become Pell-eligible. More than 50% of incarcerated adults (Davis, 2019) attempt to participate in educational opportunities provided through prison resources while incarcerated, and 79% report interest in education programs. This population could represent an untapped channel for colleges that want to improve their enrollment and provide opportunities to reduce recidivism in their communities.

A shrinking talent market

Community colleges have been brutally hit by the Great Resignation, showing a 13% staff decline from 2020-2022 due to failed searches (Shelly, 2023), difficulty filling part-time positions (Christiansen, 2022), and shortages in student services professionals (Inside Higher ED, n.d.). These gaps make it difficult to do the work that sustains healthy enrollment.

Completion

Planning helps community colleges facilitate productive conversations and develop systemwide plans to raise student completion rates substantially. The planning is initially targeted at colleges participating in the Completion by Design initiative. Based on these colleges' experiences, the planning will be revised and augmented as a living document to capture and disseminate information about improving student completion rates.

Too many students start college and do not finish. Students struggle to complete their higher education pursuits for various reasons, including lack of information and resources, financial challenges, family responsibilities, and increased costs. College completion strategies aim to help get students across the finish line and into a career by providing various financial and wraparound services to support an increase in college graduation rates.

The United States Department of Education learned that the factors most important to the success of Accelerated Study in Associate Programs include:

Remove Barriers to Full-time Attendance. Immediate financial resources remove many of the barriers to full-time attendance. These include waivers that address the gap between financial aid and tuition/fees, monthly transportation cards, and free use of textbooks. Students can then take at least 12 credits each semester and participate in winter/summer sessions to accelerate degree momentum. Students also benefit from a structured pathway with block scheduling of courses to accommodate busy schedules.

Sense of Community. Students develop a strong sense of community through the cohort approach, which encourages students to support each other and to interact regularly with faculty and staff who can act as supportive institutional agents. The special programs, such as the Accelerated Study in Associate Programs leadership program and social events, further develop students' connections to the college and one another.

Comprehensive and Coordinated Support Services. Accelerated Study in Associate Programs services is structured to address students' academic and personal growth needs. The program prioritizes staff building rapport with students so they feel comfortable discussing degree attainment challenges and successes with caring adults. Students work with the same advisor the entire time they are in the program. Students also have access to Accelerated Study in Associate Programs Career Employment Specialists to address immediate employment needs, take career assessments, develop long-term career goals and plans, and receive guidance on scholarship and opportunity programs.

Tennessee State Action

State legislators have been active in helping to remove financial barriers for students, including non-tuition costs, through strategies to provide students with food, housing, childcare, and transportation support.

Tennessee House Bill 6 (2021) creates a pilot program for completion grants for Tennessee Promise students with financial hardships. It requires the Tennessee Higher Education Commission to establish a four-year pilot program that awards grants to Tennessee Promise scholarship students who are eligible for and are receiving services as part of the college. Coaching initiatives are delivered by partnering organizations and those with immediate financial needs or experiencing financial hardships that may prevent the student from completing a postsecondary degree or credential.

Completion of Student progression.

Connection from Interest in Application Strategies

Strategy 1: Consistent college and career-ready standards

Strategy 2: Foster college-going norms supported by peers and trusted adults.

Strategy 3: Increase understanding of college requirements, application, and financial aid processes/Improve information, matching, and financial aid products

Strategy 4: Dual Enrollment/Early College High Schools Accelerated Programs

Strategy 5: Take college placement exam in High School

Strategy 6: Enrollment directly from high school

Entry from Enrollment to Completion of Success Courses

Strategy 1: Diagnostic assessment and placement

Strategy 2: Mandatory advising, attendance, life skills courses, declared courses of studies linked to career pathways

Strategy 3: Improved academic catch-up (Prevention, acceleration, supplemental instruction, concurrent enrollment, contextualization, and competency-based digital prep)

Strategy 4: Aggresstive financial aid application support

Strategy 5: Course re-design to go further, faster, and cheaper.

Progress from entry into Course of Study to 75% of requirements completed

Strategy 1: Innovative programs to incent optimal attendance.

Strategy 2: Leverage technology to make real-time feedback, intensive advising, accelerated flexibility, and student-centered learning more available.

Strategy 3: Intentional, accelerated, competency-based programs of study leading to credentials in high demands fields like STEM and healthcare

Strategy 4: Provide emergency aid to deal with unexpected life events

Completion of a program of study to credential with labor market value.

Strategy 1: Mandatory Intrusive advising

Strategy 2: Transfer with credentials incentives

Strategy 3: Remove barriers to graduation like fees and forms.

Strategy 4: Learn and Earn programs that combine attainment and work experience in a field of study toward a career pathway

Engagement

Be Intentional: Engagement does not happen by accident but by design. Most students are not on campus enough for engagement to occur spontaneously. Community colleges serve many students who juggle school, work, and family care commitments and attend college part-time. Therefore, most students typically do not benefit from spur-of-the-moment conversations about coursework or unplanned study sessions. They rarely bump into professors on campus and have serendipitous informal discussions.

Community colleges, therefore, must be deliberate and aggressively create opportunities to involve students so that engagement becomes central to every student's experience. Just as colleges must be intentional about engagement, students must be intentional about their success.

Student to Students Engagement

Throughout students' educational careers, many engagement opportunities can positively or negatively influence their lives. Even though engagement opportunities may negatively impact students' graduation and completion rates, many more factors have positively influenced degree attainment (Astin, 1993).

The number of hours spent socializing with friends, partying, student tutoring students, working on group projects, participating in intramural sports, joining a fraternity/sorority, being elected to a student office, and many others. A sense of belonging in the college community is a critical factor in student satisfaction and, therefore, can be related to student success and degree attainment. Interactions with other students have positive influences on self-esteem. An increased level of self-esteem then has a positive effect on degree attainment (Astin, 1993). Astin (1993) found that student–student interaction influences not only degree attainment and graduation but also scholarship, social activism, leadership, status striving, drive to achieve, writing ability, and emotional health (Astin, 1993, pp. 137–139).

These factors positively influence student self-esteem, persistence, and degree attainment. Astin found that living in an on-campus residence hall positively influences student retention as students are more apt to engage in activities—including peer study groups, tutoring, and class discussions—with other students in their residence halls. Living in a residence hall also helps students feel more connected to the college and allows them to make genuine connections with other students. These connections help students form positive feelings toward the college and aid in student retention (Astin, 1993; CCCSE, 2012; Espinosa, 2011; Hoffman et al., 2002; Kendricks & Arment, 2011; Reyes, 2011; Shushok & Sriram, 2010; Tinto, 1998). Astin's (1993) study noted that "practically all the involvement variables showing positive associations with retention suggest high involvement with faculty, with fellow students, or with academic work" (p. 196).

Astin (1993) concluded that a student community is one of the keys to enhancing student success in college. Students form bonds with each other and assist fellow students in personal growth, development of leadership skills, and attainment of individual goals. Astin (1993) found that lacking a student community directly impacted bachelor's degree attainment and academic development. In Student Success in College, Kuh et al. (2010) also found that the colleges selected for the DEEP (Documenting Effective Educational Practices) study all paid great attention to student–student interaction. Many colleges made specific room for peer study groups, required peer teaching, and employed peer tutors to increase their retention rates and qualify as DEEP colleges. Colleges such as Wofford College, the University of Michigan, and the University of Texas-El Paso encourage student–student engagement through study groups and peer tutoring in specific areas of the college.

They have formed student-staffed writing labs, support services, tutoring, and learning centers. Student–student engagement, primarily associated with classroom material and activities, positively influences the graduation and completion rates of many students who participate in study groups, attend learning centers, participate in intramural sports, and live in residence halls.

Student-Faculty Engagement

Many would argue that the primary function of a faculty member is to prepare the students for success in each class and eventual success in their field of choice. In the competitive and hectic times that we live in today, faculty members must also serve on numerous committees, fill administrative roles, conduct research, publish articles, and find time to enlighten and guide today's youth. Although all of these job requirements for faculty are extremely important, their influence on students' future goals, degree attainment, and persistence is often life-changing.

Student-faculty interaction has an insightful influence on student success. Many colleges and universities have insisted on intentional interaction between students and faculty members during class hours and outside the regular workday. Kuh et al. (2010) noted that many DEEP colleges make it a point to encourage, if not require, student–faculty interaction. Many DEEP colleges need their instructors to have an "open door policy" and leave their doors open while they are in the office. Many DEEP colleges also encourage undergraduate participation in faculty research projects, incorporating faculty members into peer study groups by providing areas for those groups to meet near faculty offices and calling for prompt and extensive feedback from the faculty member and the student (Kuh, 2010). Student–faculty engagement not only has a positive influence on academic attainment, but it also has a positive influence on personal growth in areas such as scholarship, social activism, leadership, status striving, drive to achieve writing ability, and emotional health (Astin, 1993, pp. 137–139). Student–faculty engagement also has a positive influence on skill development in the areas of critical thinking ability, analytical and problem-solving skills, writing skills, foreign language skills, leadership abilities, preparation for graduate or professional school, and job-related skills (Astin, 1993, pp. 236–240).

An abundance of research exists on the topic of student retention and graduation, and many articles have suggested strategies to increase retention and graduation rates. Several studies also have focused on the influence of engagement on student success, but very little research has focused on community college students. Most recent research on student engagement, especially community college student engagement, has focused on a construct-based model rather than specific engagement items that influence students' transfer intentions and STEM aspirations. A lack of research on the influence of engagement on community college students' choices to transfer and STEM aspirations and the lack of data on specific item-based engagement practices calls for further research on this topic.

References

Astin, A. W. (1993). *What matters in college: Four critical years revisited.* San Francisco: Jossey-Bass.

Brownwell, J. (2006). Meeting the competency needs of global leaders. *A partnership approach. Human Resources Management*, 45(3), 309-336.

CCCSE. (2022). *Mission Critical.* Retrieved from https://cccse.org: https://cccse.org/sites/default/files/Mission_Critical.pdf

Center for Community College Student Engagement. (2012). *A matter of degrees: Promising.* Austin, TX: University of Texas at Austin.

Christiansen, A. (2022, February 18). The Global. *COVID-19 highlights the library's struggles to fill part-time positions.*

Davis, L. M. (2019, August). Prospective. *Higher Education Programs in Prison.*

Development Dimensions International, Inc. (2020). *The Leadership Development Playbook.* Retrieved from www.ddiworld.com: https://media.ddiworld.com/ebooks/leadership-development-playbook_ebook_ddi.pdf

Evans, H. J., & Biech, E. (2018). *One hundred thirty-one ways to win accountability.* Dallas: CornerStone Leadership Institute.

Gaddam, D. S. (2021). *The leadership guide: unleashing the power within and in others.* Amazon.com.

Gentile, M. C. (2010). *Giving voice to values: How to speak your mind when you know what is right.* New Haven: Yale University Press.

Hargreaves, S. (2021). *The Compassionate Leader's Playbook.* North Somerset, UK: Sawtt.

Harris, K. (2020). *20 Proven Leadership Competencies for Emerging and Thriving Leaders.* Amazon.

Iansiti, M. (1997). Technology integration: managing technological evolution in. *Research Policy*, 521-542.

Inside Higher ED. (n.d.). Retrieved from https://www.insidehighered.com/news/2022/07/27/understanding-enrollment-declines-and-whats-ahead-key-podcast

Kouzes, J., & Posner, B. (2019). *Leadership in Higher Education.* Oakland, Berrett-Koehler Publishers.

Kuh, G. D. (2010). *Student success in college: Creating conditions that matter.* San Francisco: Jossey-Bass.

Mangan, K. (2022, October 27). The Chronicle of Higher Education. *What to Know About the New Rules on Pell Grants for Prison Education.*

Modern Psychology Publishing. (2019). *Emotional Intelligence.* Modern Psychology Publishing.

Mumford, T. C. (2007). The leadership skills strata plex: Leadership skill requirements across organizational levels. *The Leadership Quarterly*, 18, 154-166.

Schirmer, W. (2021). *The Leadership Core: Competencies for Successfully Leading Others.* New York: Morgan James Publishing.

Shelly, B. (2023, March 29). Community College Daily. *Colleges face staffing challenges.*

The Arbinger Institute. (2018). *Leadership and self-deception.* Oakland: Berrett-Koehler Publishers, Inc.

West, M. &. (1989). Innovation at work: Psychological perspectives. *Social Behavior*, 9.

William, J. W. (2021). *Communication skills training series.* Alakai Publishing LLC .

World Economic Forum. (2016). *The Future of Jobs: Employment, Skills and Workforce Strategy for the Fourth Industrial Revolution.* Geneva: World Economic Forum.